Bedford Cultur

The Commerce of Everyday Life

Selections from
THE TATLER
and THE SPECTATOR

Bedford Cultural Editions

The Commerce of Everyday Life

Selections from *The Tatler* and *The Spectator*

EDITED BY

Erin Mackie

Washington University

BEDFORD/ST. MARTIN'S   BOSTON   NEW YORK

For Bedford/St. Martin's
Developmental Editors: Katherine A. Retan and Alanya Harter
Production Editor: Lori Chong Roncka
Marketing Manager: Charles Cavaliere
Editorial Assistant: Aron Keesbury
Production Assistants: Beth Remmes and Coleen O'Hanley
Copyeditor: Linda Leet Howe
Cover Design: Terry Govan
Cover Art: Illustration of an eighteenth-century English coffeehouse, p. 14, Shelfmark X809/1645. Reproduced by permission of the British Library.
Composition: Pine Tree Composition, Inc.
Printing and Binding: R. R. Donnelley & Sons

President: Charles H. Christensen
Editorial Director: Joan E. Feinberg
Director of Editing, Design, and Production: Marcia Cohen
Managing Editor: Elizabeth M. Schaaf

Library of Congress Catalog Card Number: 97–74950

Manufactured in the United States of America.

2   1   0   9   8

f   e   d   c   b   a

For information, write: Bedford/St. Martin's, 75 Arlington Street, Boston, MA 02116 (617-426-7440)

ISBN: 0–312–11597–0   (paperback)
      0–312–16371–1   (hardcover)

Published and distributed outside North America by:

MACMILLAN PRESS LTD.
Houndmills, Basingstoke, Hampshire RG21 2XS and London
Companies and representatives throughout the world.

ISBN: 0–333–69091–5

Acknowledgments

About the Series

The need to "historicize" literary texts — and even more to analyze the historical and cultural issues all texts embody — is now embraced by almost all teachers, scholars, critics, and theoreticians. But the question of how to teach such issues in the undergraduate classroom is still a difficult one. Teachers do not always have the historical information they need for a given text, and contextual documents and sources are not always readily available in the library — even if the teacher has the expertise (and students have the energy) to ferret them out. The Bedford Cultural Editions represent an effort to make available for the classroom the kinds of facts and documents that will enable teachers to use the latest historical approaches to textual analysis and cultural criticism. The best scholarly and theoretical work has for many years gone well beyond the "new critical" practices of formalist analysis and close reading, and we offer here a practical classroom model of the ways that many different kinds of issues can be engaged when texts are not thought of as islands unto themselves.

The impetus for the recent cultural and historical emphasis has come from many directions: the so-called new historicism of the late 1980s, the dominant historical versions of both feminism and Marxism, the cultural studies movement, and a sharply changed focus in older movements such as reader response, structuralism, deconstruction, and psychoanalytic theory. Emphases differ, of course, among

schools and individuals, but what these movements and approaches
have in common is a commitment to explore — and to have students
in the classroom study interactively — texts in their full historical and
cultural dimensions. The aim is to discover how older texts (and
those from other traditions) differ from our own assumptions and ex-
pectations, and thus the focus in teaching falls on cultural and historical difference rather than on similarity or continuity.

The most striking feature of the Bedford Cultural Editions — and
the one most likely to promote creative classroom discussion — is the
inclusion of a generous selection of historical documents that contextualize the main text in a variety of ways. Each volume contains
works (or passages from works) that are contemporary with the main
text: legal and social documents, journalistic and autobiographical
accounts, histories, sections from conduct books, travel books,
poems, novels, and other historical sources. These materials have several uses. Often they provide information beyond what the main text
offers. They provide, too, different perspectives on a particular
theme, issue, or event central to the text, suggesting the range of
opinions contemporary readers would have brought to their reading
and allowing students to experience for themselves the details of cultural disagreement and debate. The documents are organized in thematic units — each with an introduction by the volume editor that
historicizes a particular issue and suggests the ways in which individual selections work to contextualize the main text.

Each volume also contains a general introduction that provides
students with information concerning the political, social, and intellectual context for the work as well as information concerning the
material aspects of the text's creation, production, and distribution.
There are also relevant illustrations, a chronology of important
events, and, when helpful, an account of the reception history of the
text. Finally, both the main work and its accompanying documents
are carefully annotated in order to enable students to grasp the significance of historical references, literary allusions, and unfamiliar
terms. Everywhere we have tried to keep the special needs of the
modern student — especially the culturally conscious student of the
turn of the millennium — in mind.

For each title, the volume editor has chosen the best teaching text
of the main work and explained his or her choice. Old spellings and
capitalizations have been preserved (except that the long "s" has been
regularized to the modern "s") — the overwhelming preference of the
two hundred teacher-scholars we surveyed in preparing the series.

Original habits of punctuation have also been kept, except for occasional places where the unusual usage would obscure the syntax for modern readers. Whenever possible, the supplementary texts and documents are reprinted from the first edition or the one most relevant to the issue at hand. We have thus meant to preserve — rather than counter — for modern students the sense of "strangeness" in older texts, expecting that the oddness will help students to see where older texts are *not* like modern ones, and expecting too that today's historically informed teachers will find their own creative ways to make something of such historical and cultural differences.

In developing this series, our goal has been to foreground the kinds of issues that typically engage teachers and students of literature and history now. We have not tried to move readers toward a particular ideological, political, or social position or to be exhaustive in our choice of contextual materials. Rather, our aim has been to be provocative — to enable teachers and students of literature to raise the most pressing political, economic, social, religious, intellectual, and artistic issues on a larger field than any single text can offer.

J. Paul Hunter, University of Chicago
William E. Cain, Wellesley College
Series Editors

About This Volume

Undertaking the reformation of polite society, *The Tatler* and *The Spectator* addressed a broad variety of topics of concern to their contemporaries and so to twentieth-century students of the eighteenth century: dressing, courtship and marriage, dueling, reading and writing, getting and spending, visiting, and the list goes on. This edition reflects the diffuse variety of these periodical papers while providing contextual material and thematic guides to help readers synthesize the papers in historical and social context. My goal here is to facilitate a reading of *The Tatler* and *The Spectator* within the full social arena from which they emerged and within which they sought the status of cultural arbiters. The themes of the chapters in this book — the market of public opinion; commerce, trade and finance; the revision of standards of taste and conduct; and the redefinition of male and female roles — are those of the papers themselves and are standing topics in eighteenth-century studies.

During the last fifty-odd years, *The Tatler* and *The Spectator* have usually been read selectively, often from one of three broad perspectives: the literary critical, the social historical, and the cultural theoretical. Within the discipline of English literary studies, the essays, mostly by Addison, on drama, taste, the imagination, Milton's *Paradise Lost*, English ballads, and true and false wit, have received some attention. But these more explicitly literary-aesthetic essays form only a single, and relatively thin, strand in the fabric of the papers as a whole. The majority focus on nonliterary topics, taking as their subject the entire scope of life as it was lived by men and women of the polite classes. This makes them useful to social historians of the period who read them as "background" material; perhaps more than any other body of text, *The Tatler* and *The Spectator* provide a wealth of information about everyday life in Queen Anne's England. The third group of readers are cultural theorists who, following the lead of the twentieth-century German social theorist Jürgen Habermas, are interested in the historical emergence and development of the "bourgeois public sphere." These theorists are interested in the papers' role in the institution of this, at once literal and symbolic, realm of public discourse in England in the early eighteenth century. Historically instrumental in the institution of the bourgeois public sphere and its new standards of conversation and conduct, *The Tatler* and *The Spectator* are not simply commentaries on their culture, but agents in its formation.

Emphasizing the uniformly *critical* and *transformative* purpose of the papers, this edition takes cues from all these dominant approaches — the literary critical, the social historical, and the cultural theoretical. Bringing these different issues together enhances our reading both of the periodicals and of the sociocultural phenomena they embody and witness. There is extensive overlap among issues we might think of as occupying different categories: the social, the ethical, the aesthetic, the commercial. This becomes apparent as we encounter "aesthetic" and "literary" concerns and vocabularies in discussions of nonliterary topics like fashion; and, conversely, literary and aesthetic topics spoken of in terms derived from the world of fashion and commerce.

The papers tend to submit all the social practices they address — dressing, gardening, talking, courting, writing, dueling — to a shared, transgeneric notion of taste. This edition, then, provides means to identify the principles of this notion of taste and to explore its broad social and historical implications. With an eye both to their historical particularity and to their great scope and variety, it situates *The Tatler* and *The Spectator* in the dynamic of cultural reformation that shaped early modern commercial society.

ACKNOWLEDGMENTS

My thinking about this book grew, in large part, out of work I did as a Ph.D. candidate with Michael McKeon. His conceptualizations of status and class and, more recently, of patriarchy and gender have informed my understanding of many of the issues thematized in this edition. Additionally, the literary-critical work of Laura Brown, Ellen Pollak, and Kathryn Shevelow and the historical-critical work on the public sphere done by Michael Warner, Nancy Fraser, and Geoff Eley have helped shape the content of this volume.

For their sympathetic and invaluable readings of the manuscript, I am grateful to Laura Brown, Lennard Davis, Robert Markley, and Beth Kowaleski-Wallace. Their guidance, along with that of Kathy Retan, my editor at Bedford/St. Martin's, helped me clarify the direction of this edition. Work on the text was expedited by the assistance of Lisa Eck, Allison Francis, Parvin Huda, and Isaac Green.

I want to thank J. Paul Hunter for inviting me to undertake this collection. The staff at Bedford has been unflaggingly supportive and patient. My thanks go, again, to my editor Kathy Retan and to Alanya Harter, who took Kathy's place later in the process. Their optimism, good sense, intelligence, and expertise helped me and the manuscript through some tricky spots. Thanks as well to the publishers, Chuck Christensen and Joan Feinberg; to Lori Roncka and Elizabeth Schaaf, who saw the manuscript through production; and to Aron Keesbury, who assisted in its compilation. For their help with office and financial matters in my department at Washington University, I extend special thanks to Judy O'Leary and Dorothy Negri.

Erin Mackie
Washington University

Contents

4. Fashioning Gender   457

Illustrations

Introduction:
Cultural and
Historical Background

In a Nation of Liberty, there is hardly a Person in the whole Mass of
the People more absolutely necessary than a Censor.
— *Tatler* No. 144 (see p. 55)

In London between 1709 and 1714, Joseph Addison and Richard
Steele published a series of fashionable and influential periodical papers, *The Tatler* and *The Spectator*. The earlier paper, *The Tatler,*
was edited, and largely written, by Richard Steele, but included con-
tributions from other authors, especially Addison, as well as correspondence from readers. *The Tatler* appeared on April 12, 1709. The
first few numbers were distributed free of charge; after that, each
issue cost one penny. Steele continued publishing *The Tatler* three
times a week until Tuesday, January 2, 1711, when the last number
appeared.

Printed in double columns on folio half-sheets of foolscap, with
advertisements at the end, *The Tatler* took the standard form of the
periodicals of the day. It stated as its explicit purpose the reformation
of manners and morals. Steele outlines the goals of the paper in his
dedication to Arthur Maynwaring, an important figure in the Whig
political party, with whom both Steele and Addison were allied: "The
general Purpose of this Paper, is to expose the false Arts of Life, to
pull off the Disguises of Cunning, Vanity, and Affectation, and to
recommend a general Simplicity in our Dress, our Discourse, and our

Behaviour" (see p. 47). And while, especially in its earlier numbers, *The Tatler* also includes more strictly news-oriented articles on current political, military, and financial events, the ethical and social focus of the paper is prominent from the start.

Although the last number of *The Tatler* appeared in January 1711, probably as a result of political pressures on Steele, this by no means marked the end of his — or Addison's — career in journalism. On March 1, 1711, the first number of *The Spectator* appeared. Whereas the editing and writing of *The Tatler* was done primarily by Steele, the production of *The Spectator* was more evenly split between the two men; this was to be a collaborative venture. Because of Addison's greater involvement, *The Spectator* came out six times a week, twice as often as *The Tatler*. The first series of *The Spectator* ran from March 1711 until December 1712 (Nos. 1–555). From June to December 1714, Addison, together with Eustace Budgell and Thomas Tickell, edited a second series, which appeared three times a week (Nos. 556–635).

Dropping those reports of current political, military, and financial news that had played a part, if an ever-diminishing one, in *The Tatler, The Spectator* largely consists of a series of self-contained, thematically unified essays. This format allows *The Spectator* more scope for the sociocultural and ethical criticism that proved the great strength and irresistible draw of *The Tatler*. The papers address a primarily, though by no means exclusively, urban audience made up of men and women in those midlevel economic and social positions that have come to be grouped under the rubric "the middle class." Taking as their subject the polite conduct of life in all its arenas, public and private, domestic and professional, social and familial, these periodicals were crucial agents in the definition of the cultural, social, and ethical ideals of that class.

The task the papers set themselves is to reform the sensibilities — aesthetic, sartorial, social, and sexual — of each man and woman in the reading audience so that he or she, guided by the principles of good sense, decorum, and benevolence, would then do, say, like, and buy the right thing. *The Tatler* and *The Spectator* wanted to enter into the daily lives of their readers and reshape them. Revealing a very modern concern with how people spend their money and their leisure time, they do not preach against consumption and pleasure per se; rather, they seek to manage these human desires in ways they consider rational, progressive, and useful, both to the individual and to the society at large. At once educational and recreational, the papers are the precursors to today's ubiquitous "life-style" magazines. *The Tatler* and *The Spectator* serve as guides, leading readers through the vast array of moral, cultural, consumer, and social choices that accompanied their relationships with one another and themselves, with the financial and commercial markets of their day, and with contemporary entertainments and pastimes. Mediating between the day-to-day social and material lives of their readers and the more universal and permanent values of good sense, honesty, modesty, decorum, and good taste, the papers attempt to secure a fixed significance for the everyday.

The success of the project depended on making the papers attractive to readers and available to the largest possible audience. These criteria are at once satisfied and complicated by the papers' status as popular, prestigious, indeed, even fashionable commodities in the market of public opinion. *The Tatler* and *The Spectator* exist within modern conditions of commodification and commercialization, which not only mark their content (the Royal Exchange, lotteries, fashions, commercial entertainments) but define their nature and shape their approach. *The Tatler* and *The Spectator* ultimately seek to manage the world from a perspective at once in and out of the world. And to be sure, the papers, like Mr. Spectator himself, exist both inside and outside the world of commerce. For although many of the objects of their reform are products of the commercialized markets of culture and fashion, and although they seek to reform the values and behavior that a commercialized society seems to encourage, the papers also derive much of their success from their status as best-sellers on the periodical market. They are themselves fashionable life-style magazines and win their place as the most prestigious arbiters of taste and manners by virtue of successful marketing. Thus, they depend upon the very commercialization and commodification they warn against.

This is perhaps the central structural paradox of the papers, and it is one that informs their strategies and ideology at almost every point. *The Tatler* and *The Spectator* do not so much repress or expel the objects of their criticism as appropriate and transform them. By championing "natural" fashions against the hoop-petticoat, the domesticated woman against the sophisticated woman of the world, the polite and aestheticized imagination against the illusions of fancy and enthusiasm, the decency of bourgeois taste against the depravity of aristocratic taste, *The Tatler* and *The Spectator* advance modern standards of British culture.

Writing at a time when cultural standards and codes of conduct were the object of much public attention, *The Tatler* and then *The Spectator* formulated signature critical styles marked by light irony and playfulness. The criticisms and prescriptions Steele and Addison advanced in each were mediated by a fictional, gently satiric persona. In *The Tatler*, Steele and Addison speak through one Isaac Bickerstaff, while *The Spectator* takes its name from Mr. Spectator, its central spokesman. Both Bickerstaff and Mr. Spectator are somewhat eccentric, self-mocking characters; their temperately satiric irony sets the witty, urbane tone.

This distinctive approach can be usefully compared to that exemplified by the Society for the Reformation of Manners and Morals, one of the most active institutions for the correction of morality at the time (see p. 115). The Society looked mostly to the lower classes and concentrated on sexual transgressions and drunkenness. Though no less devoted to standards of moderation and probity, *The Tatler* and *The Spectator* detect vice and folly in a greater range of activities and across a different spectrum of social classes. The scope of their reform is consequently broader and their attitude more worldly and liberal than that of the Society.

Backed by royal sponsorship and aristocratic support, the Society was zealous in its pursuit of offenders against decency. It regularly published blacklists of those successfully prosecuted for lewd and vicious behavior; the first thirteen of these lists contained more than ten thousand entries (Richmond Bond 71–72). In contrast, the papers usually refrain from disclosing the personal identity of those they chastise. Indeed, portraits of transgressors are of general types, not individuals. Their concern, as Addison puts it in *Spectator* No. 16, is with "the Crime as it appears in a Species, not as it is circumstanced in an Individual," and so, he refuses to publish the "Letters with private Scandal, and black Accounts of particular Persons and Families" he receives from his readers: "If I attack the Vicious, I shall only set upon them in a Body; and will not . . . make an Example of any particular Criminal" (see pp. 495–96).

More eager to reform than to expose the vicious and foolish, and always refusing to exploit sensationalist scandal, *The Tatler* and *The Spectator* approach readers not by waving the harsh rod of zealous self-righteousness, but by speaking in the congenial tones of familiar conversation. One characteristic strategy of both was to include actual and fictitious letters from readers; Steele was particularly fond of this device. *The Tatler* and *The Spectator*, then, do not simply hand down corrective moral prescriptions to an "inferior," "depraved" audience; they amiably, if sometimes ironically, engage that audience as equals in the discussion. As participants in the ongoing conversation, the audience is understood to take part in forming those standards of conduct and taste the papers champion.

Rather than depend, as did the Society for the Reformation of Manners and Morals, on legal coercion and threats of humiliating exposure, *The Tatler* and *The Spectator* rely on the subtler powers of participation and persuasion. Because they are working not simply to modify the behavior of their audience but to change their very minds, it is most important that these moral reforms be *internalized* by readers, that readers be persuaded, not coerced, into freely electing these standards of taste and behavior as their own.

AUDIENCE: NEW MANNERS FOR NEW CLASSES

It is now a commonplace that the eighteenth century witnessed the rise of the middle class in England. Social historians differ in their estimates of the size and constituency of this emergent middle class and in their assessment of its relation to other contemporary classes (titled nobility, gentry, wage laborer) and to the twentieth-century middle class. In his study of the origins of the English novel, Michael McKeon emphasizes the contradictory and mutating qualities of middle-class consciousness and ideology. The history of the middle class, writes McKeon, is marked by the presence of a simultaneous impulse "to imitate and become absorbed within the aristocracy, and to criticize and supplant not only aristocracy but status orientation itself." With, in McKeon's words, the "hindsight of modern scholarship," what we can identify as a specific middle-class orientation did not emerge as a consciously held class identity but was the result of an earlier series of attempts to reform aristocratic elite culture (*Origins* 174). McKeon and others suggest that these reformative negotiations produced the content of middle-class consciousness and ideology prior to the firm incorporation of the "middle class" as a social category.

In her work on women and popular periodicals of the early modern period, Kathryn Shevelow argues that "we can use the notion of 'middle class' to designate a particular representation of cultural values, beliefs, and practices that existed prior to, or simply apart from, their eventual conceptual coalescence into a social category" (10). Nor was the ideological work that went into the formation of what we see as "middle-class consciousness" conducted only in relation to aristocratic elite culture. As Peter Stallybrass and Allon White argue, the middle ground of bourgeois standards of taste and culture was often carved out through negotiation with "high" elite culture and "low" popular culture. In their work on eighteenth-century author-ship, they show that in bourgeois discourse these "high" and "low" cultural forms are often identified with one another and the excesses of each rejected.

Evidence from periodical subscription lists suggests that the biggest portion of their audience came from Britain's growing profes-sional bureaucracy and its commercial and financial classes; however, there is also evidence of aristocratic, and even working-class (that is, domestic servant–class), readership (Bond, *Spectator* lxxxviii–lxxxix). It is at this time that these middling and professional classes — clerks, commissioners, tradesmen, bankers, stock company directors, insur-ance financiers — begin to assume a dominant role in the nation's so-cial and cultural life as well as in its economic and political life.

Although in the early eighteenth century a comprehensive, posi-tive, and well-developed sense of middle-class identity did not yet exist, we do run across references to people who occupied the social and economic territory somewhere between the poor wage laborer and the aristocratic elite. Sometimes such references are affirmative, as in the following encomium to the middle station of life delivered to the young Robinson Crusoe by his father:

> the middle State, or what might be called the upper Station of *Low Life* . . . was the best State in the World, the most suited to human Happiness, not exposed to the Miseries and Hardships, the Labour and Sufferings of the mechanick Part of Mankind, and not embarass'd by the Pride, Luxury, Ambition and Envy of the upper Part of Man-kind. (4)

As Addison says in his eulogy on trade in *Spectator* No. 69,

> . . . there are not more useful Members in a Commonwealth than Mer-chants. They knit Mankind together in a mutual Intercourse of good Offices, distribute the Gifts of Nature, find Work for the Poor, add Wealth to the Rich, and Magnificence to the Great. . . .
>   . . . Trade, without enlarging the *British* territories, has given us a kind of additional Empire: It has multiplied the Number of the Rich, made our Landed Estates infinitely more Valuable than they were for-

merly, and added to them an Accession of other Estates as Valuable as the Lands themselves. (see p. 206)

As was widely noted, commerce could buy prestige: families could elevate themselves socially through trade and finance. Defoe celebrates this social mobility in his *Complete English Tradesman*, seeing in the rise of the commercial classes from middling to upper social ranks the potential rejuvenation of the elite, which had been corrupted by "excessive high living" and "worn out by time and family misfortunes" (see p. 279).

Such positive representations, often defensive, are attempts to revise unfavorable stereotypes of the commercial classes. The most well-developed social identity of these people was that of the "Cits" who lived in London's older districts, called "the City" to distinguish it from the newer, more fashionable districts springing up to the west. A geographical and social divide stood between the commercial classes of the City and the more elegant, often titled families who resided in the elegant squares outside the City proper. To be called a "Cit" was hardly a compliment; the commercial classes were routinely vilified for their coarse manners, low birth, and bottom-line mentality.

Pretentious, excessive, and vulgar, the taste of the modish City lady is a staple of eighteenth-century satire. The ludicrously trendy City girl is lampooned by Edward Ward in his verses on "a modish lady":

> The only daughter of some trading fop,
> Trained half in school, and t'other half in shop
> Who nothing by her parents is denied
> T'improve her charms or gratify her pride,
> Spoiled by her father's fondness and his pounds
> Till her wild fancy knows at last no bounds. (297)

And in *Spectator* No. 80, Steele presents the fashion follies of Brunetta and Phillis, two young ladies from Cheapside in the City. Exposing their vulgar desire for personal distinction, the girls engage in a series of stylistic combats that enlist all their energies and the fortunes of their families: "Their Mothers, as it is usual, engaged in the Quarrel, and supported the several Pretensions of the daughters with all that ill-chosen sort of Expence which is common with people of Plentiful Fortunes and mean Taste. The Girls preceded their Parents like Queens of *May,* in all the gaudy Colours imaginable, on every *Sunday* to Church." Assigned to a specific grid on the social map of

London — Cheapside — this sort of bad taste is linked to the class of rich yet uncultivated commercial families.

Professional men who, as well as being prominent writers, held government offices, Addison and Steele were themselves members of the middle spectrum of society. They were critics of both the proverbial vulgarity of the Cits and the stereotypical dissipation of the elite. Avoiding the defects of both, they propose principles of taste and conduct that achieve a kind of compromise between the moral demands of a more puritanical middle class and the stylistic refinement of the upper crust. As Shevelow points out, because popular periodicals like *The Tatler* and *The Spectator* aimed at an "audience relatively heterogeneous in regard to social class and educational status," they were able to mediate between the elite and the nonelite:

> Indeed, the periodicals often acted as agents for the transmission of "genteel" codes of conduct, thus aligning themselves with values explicitly associated with the upper classes. Yet they addressed readers represented as being in need of such instruction in manners. In fact, though literate and often upwardly mobile, a good segment of the intended audience for the popular periodicals, and indeed some of their editors, were and perceived themselves to be marginal to many of the practices of upper-class culture. (2–3)

This new standard for genteel society served as a way of consolidating a polite public comprising reasonable, decent people from the middle and upper classes as well as the gentry and aristocratic elite. As Terry Eagleton notes, the "major impulse" of popular periodicals like *The Tatler* and *The Spectator* "is one of class-consolidation, a codifying of the norms and regulating of the practices whereby the English bourgeoisie may negotiate an historic alliance with its social superiors" (10). Ideally, these standards of culture and conduct are "universal," and thus appropriate in any virtuous, genteel, tasteful society. They depend not on the conventional prestige markers of wealth and title, but on the less socially exclusive, more generally human principles of modesty, decorum, moderation, generosity, common sense, and good taste. These standards of identification could consequently be adopted by a broad range of classes.

The Tatler and *The Spectator* are concerned, then, not simply with championing the commercial classes but with advocating a more liberal and even "noble" use of wealth than that pursued by the typical avaricious "Cit." They formulate an identity for the businessman that combines the best features of the commercial and the noble classes.

Most simply, this involves polishing and refining the conduct of the middle classes and purging the elites of the habits of vice and folly.

Carefully differentiating between the worthy businessman and the mere "Cit" in *Tatler* No. 25, Steele contrasts two merchants, the virtuous Paulo and the base Avaro. Embodying the ideal balance of commerce and virtue, "the habitation of *Paulo* has at once the Air of a Nobleman and a Merchant. . . . His Table is the Image of Plenty and generosity, supported by Justice and Frugality." In contrast, Avaro, though one of the richest men in the City, lives "like a Beggar" and indeed is proud of his scrupulous meanness. Meditating on these two characters, Bickerstaff sums up:

> This *Paulo* . . . grows wealthy by being a common Good; *Avaro,* by being a general Evil: *Paulo* has the Art, *Avaro* the Craft of Trade. When *Paulo* gains, all Men he deals with are the better: Whenever *Avaro* profits, another certainly loses. In a Word, *Paulo* is a Citizen, and *Avaro* a Cit. (see p. 176)

Bickerstaff wants to transform Cits into citizens as valuable socially as they are economically.

Wealth is not viewed as an evil in itself, but as an advantage easily corrupted if not properly employed. The "use of riches" theme is a standard topic in social satire. In his *Epistle to Allen Lord Bathurst* (p. 266) Alexander Pope hands down a moral lesson similar to Steele's in *Tatler* No. 25:

> The Sense to value Riches, with the Art
> T'enjoy them, and the Virtue to impart,
> Not meanly, nor ambitiously pursu'd,
> Not sunk by sloth, nor rais'd by servitude;
> To balance Fortune by a just expence,
> Join with Oeconomy, Magnificence;
> With Splendor, Charity; with Plenty Health;
> Oh, teach us, Bathurst! yet unspoil'd by wealth!
> That secret rare, between th'extremes to move
> Of mad Good-nature, and of mean Self-love. (see pp. 271–72)

Many men and women were ready to take these lessons to heart. Climbing up the ladder of prestige on the rungs of commerce, finance, and politics, they were eager to acquire the social prestige and cultural polish that had traditionally been the province of the aristocracy. Thus, in the decades surrounding the turn of the eighteenth century, status-based social prestige (dependent on the inherited honors of birth) is being challenged by class-based claims (dependent on acquired wealth). The sons and daughters of wealthy India traders want cultural capital. The "Cit" wants to get "culture," to become, through wealth, status, and savoir faire, a true gentleman.

This ambition develops within the upward social migration Defoe describes: "Trade is so far *here* [in England] from being inconsistent with a Gentleman, that *in short* trade in *England* makes Gentlemen, and has peopled this nation with Gentlemen" (*Complete English Tradesman;* see p. 291). Defoe is referring to the trading families that, over the course of a generation or two, were able to make strategic marriages, to purchase estates, governmental offices, sometimes even titles, and so use commerce to finance what was, in many respects, a move out of the commercial classes and up into the gentry and aristocracy. In a more local and immediate way, the trading classes often sought to "join" the elite world through a mastery of style. One way for the tradesman to achieve the bon ton of the elite was to emulate the modes, social mores, and cultural ideals already established in the fashionable world that was still largely controlled by the aristocracy.

But this glittering beau monde of fans and fancy dress, of card games, gossip, masquerades, duels, and sexual intrigue was also discredited by those, usually outside the elite, who felt that it was morally deficient and thus no model on which to base new standards both fashionable *and* decent. The set of follies castigated by the papers — ostentation, vanity, snobbery, self-interest, insincerity, moral laxity, slavish devotion to fashion and to the modish world's empty forms — is most immediately traceable to the libertine court society of Charles II (1660–88). Preserved in the drama of the Restoration stage, with its ceaselessly witty, often ruthlessly self-serving libertine heroes and heroines, this court culture set the standard for fashionable society in the last decades of the seventeenth century. But as envisioned by Addison and Steele, genteel culture is inextricable from the fairly prosaic standards of moral virtue: modesty, benevolence, temperance, honesty, chastity before and within marriage. A fashionable society must also be a decent society. Within the flamboyant, high-style, sexually libertine culture that had carried the standard of fashion since the Restoration, these mundane, bourgeois virtues were irrelevant, even antithetical.

In his description of the pursuits of the three brothers in *A Tale of a Tub,* Jonathan Swift neatly outlines the course of life to which the fashionable Restoration man-about-town aspired:

They Writ, and Raillyed, and Rhymed, and Sung, and Said, and said
Nothing: They Drank, and Fought, and Whor'd, and Slept, and Swore,
and took Snuff: They went to New Plays on the first Night, haunted
the *Chocolate*-Houses, beat the Watch, lay on Bulks, and got Claps:
They bilkt Hackney-Coachmen, ran in Debt with Shop-keepers, and
lay with their Wives: They kill'd Bayliffs, kick'd Fidlers down Stairs,
eat at *Locket's* [a chic restaurant], loytered at *Will's* [a literary coffee-
house]. (45)

Fashionable society too often neglected virtue, true honor, common
sense, and good taste in favor of the patently illicit code of conduct
followed by the libertine and the ostentation of the modish fop and
coquette. The Restoration rake is epitomized in Dorimant, the pro-
tagonist of George Etherege's *The Man of Mode* (1676). Charming,
articulate, and predatory, Dorimant is a social and sexual barracuda
who embodies the stylized amorality and chic cynicism that characterized the Stuart court. Dorimant's seductive charisma, generated
largely by his verbal mastery, is registered in one character's observation: "Oh, he has a tongue, they say, would tempt the angels to a second fall" (3.3.115–16).

Sir Fopling Flutter, in the same play, incarnates the qualities of
that other (and, as Etherege suggests, related) Restoration type, the
fop. Affected, full of substanceless conversation peppered with
French tags, dressed in the latest Parisian fashion, Sir Fopling Flutter
is judged harshly by his peers: "A fine-mettled coxcomb"; "Brisk and
insipid — "; "Pert and dull" (3.2.241–43). Yet as the perceptive
Emilia points out, he is nonetheless able to purchase a good deal of
social prestige with his French style: "However you despise him, gentleman, I'll lay my life he passes for a wit among many" (3.2.245).
The open question of Etherege's play is whether Sir Fopling or Dorimant is the *true* "Man of Mode." The gentleman of fashion is either
a ruthless, amoral rake (Dorimant) or a contemptible, witless fop
(Fopling). Against such a dismal choice Steele and Addison propose
an alternative ideal, that of the refined man of taste and urbane address who is neither libertine nor fop. In *Spectator* No. 65, Steele
counters the ethical possibilities presented by *The Man of Mode*.
Noting with disapproval that "the received Character of the Play is,
That it is the Pattern of Gentile Comedy," Steele attempts to dislodge
it and its cast of characters from this exemplary status. According to
Steele, the hero Dorimant, far from being a gentleman, "is a direct
Knave in his Designs" and "more of a Coxcomb than . . . *Foplin*";
the heroine, Harriet, lacks proper respect for her mother; and the

play as a whole displays an utter "Negligence of every thing, which engages the Attention of the sober and valuable Part of Mankind" (see p. 367).

More generally, however, the sober virtues valued by the papers were neglected not simply by rakes, fops, and coquettes but by more temperate men and women, who also followed fashion's dictates in order to maintain their social standing. Thus the entirely innocuous young lady in *Tatler* No. 116 has succumbed to the extravagant and irrational new fad, the hoop-petticoat. She explains "that she had a Mind to look as big and burly as other Persons of her Quality; That she had kept out of it as long as she could, and till she began to appear little in the Eyes of all her Acquaintance" (see p. 483).

This emulation of fashion for fashion's sake had repercussions beyond the choice of dress. In the early eighteenth century, as today, there were well-established human social types that set the pattern for both the style of clothes it was fashionable to wear and the sort of person it was fashionable to be. In his discussion of the character of the rake, Steele cites those young men, themselves not especially dissolute by nature, who nonetheless pose as rakes simply because the rake is a fashionable, popular character type (*Tatler* No. 27; see p. 471). One such (reformed) poseur writes a letter published in *Spectator* No. 154 complaining that he received little respect in the beau monde until he began a course of conspicuous, stylized dissipation: then, "in due Process of Time I was a very pretty Rake among the Men, and a very pretty Fellow among the Women" (p. 521). In his natural character as "a sober modest Man," he "was always looked upon by both Sexes as a precise unfashioned Fellow of no Life or Spirit" (see p. 520). Addison and Steele want to change social standards so that what is sober, sensible, and modest is also fashionable. They want fashionable society to be more responsive to standards of ethical decency.

That their project met with considerable immediate success, at least in some quarters, is witnessed by the reader's comments published in *Spectator* No. 461:

> Give me Leave therefore to do you Justice, and say in your Behalf . . . That Modesty is become fashionable. . . . Prophaneness, Lewdness, and Debauchery are not now Qualifications, and a Man may be a very fine Gentleman, tho' he is neither a Keeper [of women] nor an Infidel.

In his *Present State of Wit,* John Gay commends Bickerstaff on the success of his reform:

'Tis incredible to conceive the effect his Writings have had on the Town; How many Thousand follies they have either quite banish'd, or given a very great check to; how much Countenance they have added to vertue and Religion; how many People they have render'd happy, by shewing them it was their own fault if they were not so; and lastly, how intirely they have convinc'd our Fops and Young Fellows, of the value and advantages of Learning. (see p. 152)

Noting the profound change in codes of civil behavior to which *The Tatler* and *The Spectator* contributed, the twentieth-century English man of letters C. S. Lewis remarked that the "sober code of manners under which we still live today, is in some important degree a legacy from the *Tatler* and the *Spectator.*" What we unthinkingly accept as natural social behavior was in its time a revolution: "There was a real novelty in the new manners" (7).

One important difference is the marked departure of these new manners from a kind of violently hyperbolic expression. Addison and Steele want to attain a more civil, peaceable standard of style and manners than that epitomized by those would-be wits and gallants, who mistake extravagant violence and violent extravagance for elegance and aplomb. Features of the bad old manners can be seen in Bickerstaff's description of what once passed for stylish pastimes among rakes:

When I was a middle-ag'd Man, there were many Societies of ambitious young Men in *England*, who, in their Pursuits after Fame, were every Night employ'd in roasting Porters, smoaking Coblers, knocking down Watchmen, overturning Constables, breaking Windows, blackening Sign-Posts, and the like immortal Enterprizes, that dispers'd their Reputation throughout the whole Kingdom. One could hardly finc a Knocker at a Door in a whole Street after a midnight Expedition of these *Beaux Esprits*. (*Tatler* No. 77)

"I am inclined to think," remarks Lewis, "that if we saw it now we should mistake that [older sort of] high breeding for no breeding at all": "The walk of the courtier would seem to us a Janissary's strut, his readiness to find quarrel in a straw would seem a yokel touchiness, his clothes an intolerable ostentation" (7). The "readiness to find quarrel in a straw" comes from allegiance to an archaic, aristocratic code of honor, which held on in a number of forms through the eighteenth century. The duel is perhaps the most notable of these and an institution Steele avidly campaigns against in *Tatler* Nos. 25, 26, 28, and 29. Highlighting the absurdity of this self-destructive ritual of honor, in *Tatler* No. 25 Steele produces a parodic letter in which one gentleman "demands satisfaction" from another:

Sir,

Your extraordinary Behaviour last Night, and the Liberty you were pleas'd to take with me, makes me this Morning give you this, to tell you, because you are an ill-bred Puppy, I will meet you in *Hide*-Park an Hour hence; and because you want both Breeding and Humanity, I desire you would come with a Pistol in your Hand, on Horseback, and endeavour to shoot me through the Head, to teach you more Manners. If you fail of doing me this Pleasure, I shall say, You are a Rascal on every Post in Town: And so, Sir, if you will not injure me more, I will never forgive what you have done already. . . .

Sir,

Your Most Obedient

Humble Servant, &c. (see pp. 470–71)

Other, somewhat more muted manifestations of the same flamboyant culture of personal prestige are apparent in the overstylized social forms and modes of dress and manners on display among a wide swathe of society — beaux, fops, coquettes, smart-fellows, prettyfellows, female "idols" (fashion divas), and so on. So artificial has the standard of elegance become that stylish people adopt limps and lisps and nervous disorders as their own: there has arisen among fashionable men and women "a kind of inverted Ambition" to "affect even Faults and Imperfections of which they are Innocent" (*Tatler* No. 77). Addison and Steele want to return people to their senses and institute a mode of life more moderate, composed, and natural.

Approaching their reform in the spirit of liberal guidance rather than puritanical castigation, Addison and Steele do not ask for an abandonment of fashion, wit, and fancy — those stylizing forms of dress, thought, language, and behavior that give elegance and polish to social life and literature — but for a rethinking of the terms themselves. What, they ask, is true and what false wit? What is the difference between elegance and affectation? What, then, is good taste? Who qualifies as a fine gentleman? How might what is fashionable, witty, and elegant be made compatible with what is ethically sound and socially responsible?

· COFFEEHOUSES, PERIODICALS,
AND THE PUBLIC SPHERE

Popular print culture became a central institution for defining and disseminating genteel, bourgeois cultural standards. There was at this period a growing (though still tiny) literate public with enough education, money, leisure, and interest to make reading a part of their daily lives. The success of popular journals like *The Tatler* and *The Spectator,* at once "improving" and entertaining, bears testimony to a public who not only could read but chose to read in their free time. The growing role of literature as a popular pastime is reflected in the rise of the modern novel, whose relative educational and recreational functions were hotly disputed, the full-flowering of the periodical press, and, in general, an expanding market for all kinds of printed material.

By the early eighteenth century the writing and printing of books and periodicals were a well-established business. The older system of literary patronage, in which aristocratic supporters provided authors with financial and social backing, was giving way to a more purely commercial mode of operation. Addison and Steele take their rightful places within the emerging profession of commercial writers. But the lucrative popular press provoked considerable reaction from those who saw it as an agent of cultural corruption. This reaction typically took the form of satires against "Grub Street hacks," desperate, unskilled men who wrote to earn enough money simply to scrape by, with no thought of the value or quality of their work. But at the same time, considerable counterclaims were being made for the high quality and respectability of the popular press. Through the commercial culture industry that developed during this time, writing and printing themselves assume the status of middle-class professions.

An institution central to the organization of public life in early-eighteenth-century London, the coffeehouse is closely affiliated with the authors, audience, aims, and accomplishments of popular periodicals like *The Tatler* and *The Spectator*. In its initial number, *The Tatler* confirms this connection by announcing its various departments:

> All Accounts of *Gallantry, Pleasure,* and *Entertainment,* shall be under the Article of *White's Chocolate-house; Poetry,* under that of *Will's Coffee-house; Learning,* under the Title of *Graecian; Foreign* and *Domestick News,* you will have from St. *James's Coffee-house;* and what else I have to offer on any other Subject, shall be dated from my own *Apartment.* (see p. 50)

As we see here, Steele divides his subject matter by assigning it different discrete sections, each emanating from the specific place — coffeehouse, chocolate house, or private apartment — where that topic is most likely to be discussed. The paper's design thus traces

London's social geography: its departments stand as newsprint analogues of actual places, public and private.

The Tatler's relationship to the coffeehouse is double-faceted: not only was it generated from these public resorts of business and talk, it was also largely read there. Papers like *The Tatler* and *The Spectator* were written to be talked about. The essays enter a cultural debate that was highly oral and social rather than textual and academic, and coffeehouses were the chief sites of this debate. Some functioned as clearinghouses for the latest military, political, or economic news; others, like Man's, were fashionable resorts where beaus met to pose and gossip; still others, like Will's, were oriented around literary culture and served as critical tribunals. Coffeehouses were crucial arenas for the formation and expression of public opinion about plays and poetry, politics and finance, dress and manners. An author's reception at Will's could make or break a reputation. The stereotypical theater critic, Sir Timothy Tittle, whose mission it is to "[put] Men in Vogue, or [condemn] them to Obscurity," laughs to scorn any author not known there (*Tatler* No. 165; see p. 340). Of course, the formation of public opinion is the first object of the papers. So it is in the coffeehouse culture that *The Tatler* locates its origins, its aims, and its audience.

First established in London in the mid–seventeenth century, coffeehouses multiplied at a remarkable rate; by the end of the century there were more than two thousand of them in the city (Stallybrass and White 95). The coffeehouse and the popular periodicals patrons read and discussed there are two institutions central to that arena of discourse and identification Jürgen Habermas calls the "bourgeois public sphere." Habermas's bourgeois public sphere is at once a symbolic space and a literal space for the production of that set of ideological and social ideals we have come to identify with the polite middle class. It encompasses both the public discursive spheres of the newspaper and the coffeehouse and the set of normative principles defined in these arenas. Ideally an open forum of rational discussion, the bourgeois public sphere emerging in early eighteenth-century England served a number of significant functions: it was an arena of social identification for individuals; it provided standards for interaction and public discussion; it established rationales for ever more secularized and commercialized modes of cultural production; and it stood as a place outside official state power from which criticism against the state could be launched.

Through the networks of institutions like the press and the coffee-house a new notion of the "public" arose, one that was composed of private individuals who came together to debate and negotiate matters of public concern, to formulate "public opinion." Represented to itself through the press, this new "public of the now emerging *public sphere of civil society*" becomes aware of itself as a source of authority and validation separate from, and even opposed to, state authority. Operating "as a forum in which the private people, come together to form a public, readied themselves to compel public authority to legitimate itself before public opinion," the public sphere had political uses (Habermas 25–26).

Public opinion also developed around ethical, social, and aesthetic-cultural issues. The public sphere is first and foremost a critical arena where individuals take part in a debate about the principles, interests, aims, and standards that ought to govern their political, social, ethical, and aesthetic-cultural lives. Largely through publications like *The Tatler* and *The Spectator,* the public sphere becomes the "place" where the cultural and social norms of bourgeois modernity are instituted. By identifying themselves with these sets of norms, and so internalizing them, the bourgeoisie establishes its own social identity. Initially an arena of identification and debate for the commercial classes, the bourgeois public sphere gradually encompasses a wider spectrum of the status and class hierarchy. It is able to serve such a social function because, theoretically at least, in the public sphere discrepancies of wealth and status are rendered inoperative.

Claiming a broad-based consensus among all "rational human beings," the authority of the bourgeois public sphere is based on the abstract principles of nature, justice, sense, and beauty. Ideally, anyone can claim access to this sphere of public debate. In *Tatler* No. 225, Bickerstaff articulates the principles later identified by Habermas as those of the bourgeois public sphere, where access is bought with the currency of good sense, benevolence, and reason:

> Equality is the Life of Conversation. . . . Familiarity in Inferiors is Sauciness; in Superiors, Condescension; neither of which are to have Being among Companions, the very Word implying that they are to be equal. When therefore we have abstracted the Company from all Considerations of their Quality or Fortune, it will immediately appear, that to make it happy and polite, there must nothing be started which shall discover that our Thoughts run upon any such Distinctions. (see p. 343)

As front-runners in the establishment of the bourgeois public sphere, *The Tatler* and *The Spectator* carve out a public social space where traditional status and wealth hierarchies are rendered irrelevant by the more egalitarian standards of abstract human rationality. In their pages, members of the gentry and aristocrats may sit down with tradesmen and financiers and pursue rational conversation. It is on the common ground of the bourgeois public sphere that the consolidation of elite and commercial, professional classes, of high and middle, can take place.

This discussion of the public sphere should, of course, be punctuated with the equivocating term "ideal" to suggest that its actual operation somehow differed from its ostensible aims of universality and inclusiveness. Complicating the claims made by Habermas, Stallybrass and White emphasize the historical, ideological, and topographical particularities that characterize the public sphere, pointing to all that it excludes and displaces. The public sphere, they argue, is a notion embedded in a specific kind of urban space, the exclusively male coffeehouses and clubs of London. These venues demanded particular standards of behavior and fostered specific sorts of discussion. The polite, conversation-oriented conduct of the coffeehouses departed from the raucous, alcohol-charged style of social interaction that characterized the alehouses and taverns, which the coffeehouses to some extent displaced in terms of prestige and social centrality. Where the tavern and alehouse were sites for release and nonproductive leisure, the coffeehouse offered a milieu of considerable restraint, rational debate, and productive leisure. In the alehouse one resorted to a realm of pleasure removed from the demands of work; in the coffeehouse, pleasure never abandoned business. As Stallybrass and White note, the "coffeehouse has a habit of metamorphosizing into professional or business institutions" (99). What the coffeehouses excluded were the "intoxication, rhythmic and unpredictable movements, sexual reference and symbolism, singing and chanting, bodily pleasures and 'fooling around'" that were the order of the day at the neighborhood tavern or alehouse (97).

As people conformed to these new codes of conduct, cultivated this sort of discourse, and, especially, internalized the ideology within which such conduct and conversation appear "natural" and "inevitably" right, they became, in an important sense, different people — the kind of people at home in coffeehouse society. The public sphere can thus be understood less as accommodating an inclusive and universal class of humankind than as producing a quite specific sort of person with the peculiar conviction that he represents a universal class of humanity.

SEXUAL DIFFERENCE, SOCIAL SPHERES, AND GENDERED IDENTITY

The Tatler and *The Spectator* are intent on cultivating an audience who will act in ways suitable to the genteel and rational exchange of the coffeehouse, but they are also concerned with conduct and employment in the more private sphere of the domestic household. Designed for consumption both in the male-oriented, public and social venues of the coffeehouse and club and at the tea tables presided over by the ladies of the house, these papers undertake the direction of both public and private life. As Shevelow explains, the popular periodical performed an important transaction between the public and private spheres: "The periodical was a public disseminator of prescriptions for private behavior; it constructed, for public consumption, normative images of 'private life' closely identified with women" (4).

In the late seventeenth and early eighteenth centuries, the social geography was changing. As Ellen Pollak outlines in her discussion of the eighteenth-century feminine ideal, upper- and middle-class women increasingly withdrew from the arenas of economic productivity into the domestic realm of consumption, partly in emulating their aristocratic superiors. Ensconced in the home, sequestered from the "corrupt" worlds of politics, finance, and commerce, women become "the embodiment of moral value" that infuses domestic space (42). Women start to take on the role of angels in the house, custodians of moral and spiritual life.

What emerges in the eighteenth century is an increasingly polarized separation of spheres: public/social/masculine versus private/familiar/feminine. The way this separation is naturalized depends on an early modern shift in the understanding of sexual difference, on the notion that the masculine and the feminine are themselves polar opposites and that this opposition is rooted in natural difference. Gender, the cultural marks of maleness and femaleness, is increasingly seen as biologically innate rather than socially secured. McKeon notes that "in the later seventeenth and eighteenth centuries, England acquired the modern wisdom that there are not one but two sexes; that they are defined not by behavior, which is variable, but by nature, which is not" ("Historicizing Patriarchy" 301).

As inheritors of this naturalized, sexualized notion of gender difference, we need reminding that this notion is truly a modern one. Previously, gender difference was hierarchical rather than oppositional: men and women were understood to be constructed along the same lines, even in terms of their sexual organs, but female anatomy was a less efficient, second-tier copy of male anatomy. Gender, then, is produced not so much by the sexual differences with which we are born (sexual differences rooted in biology were not recognized as such) as by the socially recognized signs of difference — behavior, dress, hairstyle, occupation, social position (Laqueur 149–53).

Indeed, there is considerable reason to believe that before the modern period, the dominant identity category was not gender but status, for within a society structured around inherited honors, differences in status seem most natural, inherent, and inevitable (McKeon, "Historicizing Patriarchy" 304–05). In the old aristocratic order, a person is first and foremost either a noble or a commoner. But as economic-oriented class differences begin to challenge the hold of status on social prestige, the system of cultural differences that define identity finds its fixed point in gender. One may well be a noble or a commoner, but one is first and foremost either a man or a woman. Accordingly, as the crucial sign of a person's identity, the signs of gender difference become vexed with more anxiety and urgency than the signs of status difference. The eighteenth century is increasingly occupied with the regulation of gender norms, with policing gender transgressions (such as cross-dressing), and with making sure that men and women confine themselves to their proper spheres, men in the public, social world, women in the private, domestic realm.

This model of sexual difference, and its attendant anxieties and preoccupations, is fully at work in *The Tatler* and *The Spectator*. Female readers are addressed first "*as women,* with class associations more vaguely assumed in the rhetoric directed toward them" (Shevelow 23). This is yet another way the popular periodicals reached an audience that cut across class and status lines: their address to the "ladies" speaks to women in the commercial and professional classes, the gentry, and the aristocracy. According to the ideology of gender at work in *The Tatler* and *The Spectator,* women form a distinct social category defined solely by their innate female nature. This inherent and inalterable feminine nature could find its proper expression and direction only within the domestic, private sphere. The good female characters are those who cheerfully confine themselves to the concerns of their families. Excessively worldly women whose interests and occupations range beyond the private household represent a kind of "bad femininity," which the papers do their best to discourage. These badly feminine women think more of card games and masquerades than of household tasks; they are preoccupied with public social display rather than the well-being of their family circle; immodest, even exhibitionist, they strive after social power and pose the threat of sexual autonomy.

The handing down of normative prescriptions for women forms a central focus of both papers. Although immersed in the exclusively masculine culture of the coffeehouses, even *The Tatler* by no means limited its scope to purely masculine affairs or addressed itself solely to men. In the first number Steele claims that a dominant purpose of the paper is to provide "something which may be of Entertainment to the Fair Sex." In a compliment more than a little backhanded, he reports that he has named his paper *The Tatler* specifically in honor of the ladies (see pp. 49–50). To tattle is to gossip, and women in the eighteenth century, as today, are mocked for their supposed addiction to this form of conversation. In *The Tatler* that "private and scandal-mongering activity traditionally figured as a predominately feminine vice" is transformed into an "agent of reform" (Shevelow 93).

Steele's gallant, gently mocking nod to the fair sex signals an attention to women actively maintained throughout the publication of both *The Tatler* and *The Spectator*. Women warrant this constant regard by virtue of their peculiar, sex-linked weaknesses of character. Addison elaborates on the "light, fantastical Disposition" of women in *Spectator* No. 15, citing at length the ways in which their natural female weakness for whatever is superficial and trivial makes women the particular dupes of fashion and meaningless social forms. Women are the very incarnation of those affectations and follies the papers campaign against. So greatly do women overvalue appearances, and so narrowly do they limit their thoughts and discussions to "the Drapery of the Species," that they are in danger of falling in love with the clothes rather than the man. Any girl brought up in the usual ways of fashionable society is likely, Mr. Spectator asserts, to be in love with "every Embroidered Coat that comes in her Way," and ruinously seduced by "a Pair of fringed Gloves" (see pp. 491–92).

If their natural frailty makes them more vulnerable to such misguided affections, women's nurture and upbringing also does little to strengthen their character. Bickerstaff and Mr. Spectator object to conventional female education because, they claim, it promotes aspirations toward social status achieved through self-display and so fosters a race of worldly, exhibitionist women who value themselves and others wholly on externals. Advocates of female modesty and retirement from the public world, Addison and Steele promote a program of female education that cultivates attention to internal beauty and to a woman's strictly domestic, familial social obligations. Steele gives a "short Rule for [female] Behavior" in *Spectator* No. 104: "every young Lady in her Dress, Words, and Actions [should] recommend her self as a Sister, Daughter, or Wife, and make her self the more esteemed in one of those Characters."

Female nature is innately frivolous and unstable. Since these qualities are understood as natural and inalterable, the schemes of female reform and education proposed in the papers encounter a problem. For even as they are being enlisted as symbols of the realm of domestic virtue, women are also understood to lack the native stability that would most effectively allow them to resist the sway of the world's temptations. Women seem naturally flawed in ways that threaten the realization of what is being defined as their natural character. Jane Spencer remarks on this contradiction: "It seems that eighteenth-century women needed a good deal of educating into their 'inborn,' 'natural' feminine qualities" (15). As they define and prescribe these normative qualities, *The Tatler* and *The Spectator* reveal, with remarkable clarity, the construction of modern gender norms in process.

POLITICS, PERIODICALS, AND PERSONAE

Although, especially in *The Spectator,* Addison and Steele seem chiefly concerned with the direction of ethical, social, and cultural, rather than political and economic life and at times pointedly distance themselves from common newsmongers, the scarcity of explicitly political content must not be misunderstood as the absence of political position. Both men held office in Whig governments and both advocated the sociocultural views associated with that party, its constituents, and their interests.

Engineers of the funded National Debt and the Bank of England (1694), which provided the government loans necessary for England to pursue its wars against the French, the Whigs worked in alliance with the London mercantile and financial establishment. As a party, the Whigs had emerged along with their oppositional counterparts, the Tories, from alliances formed, respectively, for and against the exclusion of James II from the throne in 1679. The Whigs supported the right of Parliament to exclude James on the basis of his Catholic religion, while the Tories insisted on his hereditary rights as the brother of King Charles II, despite his Catholicism. From the Exclusion crisis through the first third of the eighteenth century, opposition between Whigs and Tories defined the English political map. Identified largely with the Anglican squirearchy, the Tories were less religiously tolerant than the Whigs, and, unlike the Whigs, highly mistrustful of William III's expensive course of foreign conflicts, the Nine Years War (1689–96) and the War of the Spanish Succession (1701–14), which continued under Queen Anne. The Whigs represented a coalition of the interests of aristocratic landowning families with the financial interests of the middle classes. By their enemies, Tories were suspected of Jacobism (support of Stuart claimants to the throne on whose behalf rebellions were launched in 1715 and 1745), with its treasonous Papist and French sympathies; the Whigs were maligned by theirs for their devotion to financial and commercial interests and (especially later under the ministry of Robert Walpole, 1721–42) for politicizing government appointments and corrupting the political process with bribes, gerrymandering, graft, and other dubious modes of influence-mongering.

A close associate of the great Whig party leaders and member of the prominent Whig Kit-Cat Club, Addison held various government offices and performed diplomatic duties until the fall of the Whigs in 1710. In 1714, with the death of Queen Anne and the resurgence of the Whig party, Addison again entered political life and was appointed a lord commissioner of trade. Steele joined King William's army in its campaigns against the French during the Nine Years War and served from 1692–1705. As a journalist for Whig interests, Steele authored the *London Gazette* and held a post as commissioner of stamps; in 1710 when the Whigs fell from power, he lost the *Gazette* but held on to his commissionership. Even more than Addison's, Steele's career centered heavily on party politics; Steele was elected to Parliament twice, first in 1713 and again in 1715.

The Whigs were staunchly anti-Papist and anti-French, dedicated adherents of constitutional monarchy, energetic advocates of England's imperialist designs, and eager promoters of the financial and commercial powers that fueled and profited from those designs. And even where political concerns are not at issue, the Whig ideology comes through in the papers loud and clear in their associations, allusions, and rhetorical figures. The anti-French and anti-Papist bias that characterizes Whig political ideology gets translated by Addison and Steele into the extrapolitical arenas of taste and manners. This transformation politicizes the content of their aesthetic and ethical discussions even as it fashions the cultural and aesthetic identity of a particular political ideology. In *Spectator* No. 119, where he discusses the new mode of natural manners, Addison compares this reform in standards of personal style to the Protestant Reformation: "Conversation, like the *Romish* Religion, was so encumbered with Show and Ceremony, that it stood in need of a Reformation to retrench its Superfluities, and restore it to its natural good Sense and Beauty" (see p. 513). In *Spectator* No. 45, Addison explicitly refers to the war (and to rumors that the Tories were secretly negotiating for peace) but only in the context of a discussion of female fashion. Somewhat tongue-in-cheek, he professes a desire for "a safe and honourable Peace." He immediately goes on to voice his fears that this would end the embargo on French goods and so open the floodgates to an "Inundation of Ribbons and Brocades" and to propose "an Act of Parliament for Prohibiting the Importation of *French* Fopperies."

In *The Tatler* and *The Spectator,* the superficial, superfluous, artificial, delusive, showy, pretentious, and affected are explicitly associated with the French court and the Roman Catholic religion. This association also takes in the Francophile court of Charles II and, by extension, any regressive or outmoded adherence to the forms, manners, and modes of that court. Moreover, the persistence of these forms becomes identified with the residual presence in English society of Jacobite sympathies. The reformation of manners and mores undertaken by Addison and Steele, as the example cited above shows, is seen as a progressive movement that discounts and discards the forms and ceremonies of the earlier age, not simply because they are superfluous encumbrances, but because they bear the stamp of Papist, French, and Jacobite sympathies, of absolutism, of everything England had been at war with for the previous two decades. In a sense, then, *The Tatler* and *The Spectator,* both wartime publications, translate the ongoing political and military battles against the French onto the domestic and social theater of a cultural war.

The Tatler and *The Spectator* are heirs to the market of news and opinion that grew to profusion from the mid–seventeenth century on, fueled by the greater demand for news bearing on England's commercial and financial markets and by the debates surrounding the political upheavals of the Civil Wars, the Restoration, the Glorious Revolution, and all their attendant renegotiations of sovereign prerogative, of the relations between church and state, and of the foreign and domestic policy that bore on England's expanding colonial and commercial interests. Since the mid–seventeenth century the market in periodicals had continued to swell, especially after the lapse of the Licensing Act in 1695, which ended statutory censorship of the press. Throughout the eighteenth century, men and women of letters were often journalists: Daniel Defoe, for example, the author of *Moll Flanders* and *Robinson Crusoe*, for nine years single-handedly wrote his *Review*; Jonathan Swift wrote the Tory *Examiner*; the fiction writer Mary de la Rivière Manley was an author of *The Female Tatler*; later in the century, the critic, biographer, and lexicographer Samuel Johnson had his *Rambler*; the playwright and novelist Henry Fielding wrote *The Champion, The True Patriot,* and *The Jacobite Journal*; and the poet, playwright, and novelist Oliver Goldsmith penned *The Bee* and *The Busy Body*.

Although *The Tatler* and *The Spectator* quickly won and tenaciously held on to their position of prominence amid the myriad periodicals of the day, little about them is categorically new or unique: other periodicals published fiction along with essays and new reports and incorporated letters from readers, and certainly there were already journals of opinion. *The Tatler* follows an established tradition of mixing essays with sections of news, as did the *Gentleman's Journal*, the *Post-Angel*, the *Diverting Post*, and the *British Apollo*. *The Tatler* and *The Spectator* contain poems and fictional tales, but other periodicals, like the *Monthly Miscellany*, and again, the *Gentleman's Journal*, also functioned as literary miscellanies.

Two features that do perhaps distinguish *The Tatler* and then *The Spectator* from the scores of other early eighteenth-century periodicals are their well-developed and continuous fictional personae, Isaac Bickerstaff and Mr. Spectator, and their refinement of the single-essay format. For it is as essayists that Steele and, even more, Addison, are respected by literary historians. *The Spectator* especially represents a watershed in the stylistic development of the English occasional essay, setting a standard emulated throughout the following century. In his *English Literature and Society in the Eighteenth Century*, Leslie Stephen emphasizes the ongoing influence of Addison and Steele:

> *The Spectator* became the model for at least three generations of writers. The number of imitations is countless: Fielding, Johnson, Goldsmith, and many men of less fame tried to repeat the success; persons

of quality, such as Chesterfield and Horace Walpole, condescended to write papers for the *World*. . . . Even in the nineteenth century Hazlitt and Leigh Hunt carried on the form; as indeed, in a modified shape, many later essayists have aimed at a substantially similar achievement. (70–71)

And in the famous closing lines of his *Life of Addison*, Samuel Johnson remarks, "Whoever wishes to attain an English style, familiar but not coarse, and elegant but not ostentatious, must give his days and nights to the volumes of Addison" (440).

As Stephen notes, a number of imitators sprang up in the wake of the *Tatler*'s and *Spectator*'s success, English, French, German, Dutch, and eventually even Polish and Russian. There were, as well, the inevitable pirated editions and publications put forward by nameless hack writers in Bickerstaff's name. In *Tatler* No. 229 Addison reflects on "those numberless Vermin that feed upon this Paper . . . I mean, the small Wits and Scribblers that every Day turn a Penny by nibbling at my Lucubrations" (see p. 74).

Rather than pose any real threat, these numerous competitors and imitators simply bear witness to the health of the periodical market. *The Tatler* and *The Spectator* were undertaken to provide an expressive channel for Steele's and Addison's social and cultural criticism, and to turn a profit, to sell that criticism on what proved to be the solidly lucrative market of public opinion. Without financial backing from either private patron or government, *The Tatler* and *The Spectator* were purely commercial enterprises, funded solely by sales and advertisements. They paid their authors well from daily sales and from the successful collected editions that appeared, simultaneously, first in monthly and then in more comprehensive volumes. Such popular success later spurred Steele and Addison on to other periodical pursuits: Steele's *Guardian* and Addison's *The Freeholder* are the most significant.

The status that their contemporaries and posterity have granted to *The Tatler* and *The Spectator* over and above other periodicals is fully in line with Steele's and Addison's own estimations. Both Bickerstaff and Mr. Spectator are eager to distinguish themselves from the common run, claiming for their papers superior subject matter and a surer hold on truth, taste, and reason. From early on, *The Tatler* defines itself in opposition to exclusively news-oriented journalism like the *Gazette*, which Steele edited concurrently with *The Tatler*. In his first essay for *The Tatler* (No. 18), Addison addresses the difference between this and other newspapers, distinguishing himself from "the ingenious Fraternity" of news journalists. His interests, his field of operation, his material — all differ from those of the common run of newshounds who, during the War of the Spanish Succession, were mostly chasing after war stories. While they pursue "Camps, Fortifications, and Fields of Battle," Bickerstaff covers another territory, a land of urban and domestic culture where the "chief Scenes of Action are Coffee-houses, Play-houses, and my own Apartment." In an early issue of *The Spectator* (No. 10), Addison claims that the content of his paper bears a closer and more valuable relation to its audience than any newspaper: "Is it not much better to be let into the Knowledge of ones-self, than to hear what passes in *Muscovy* or *Poland?*" (see p. 89).

By calling his own paper *The Tatler* and so identifying it with a form of social discourse he associates with female triviality, Steele, as Bickerstaff, places his whole reformative enterprise within a self-ironizing framework. The title and its self-mocking, ironical tone signal a set of closely related statements about itself and its strategies. It suggests, first, that *The Tatler,* for all its reformative intent, is not tediously didactic and prescriptive, but entertaining, a playful contribution to that ongoing urban conversation, the town talks pursued at the polite tea-tables and coffeehouses throughout the city. To suggest that its contents are mere "tattling" draws attention away from the seriousness of *The Tatler*'s purpose. The paper and its persona thus eschew any overtly authoritarian role and establish a relationship of compassionate camaraderie with the audience.

Bickerstaff fosters an intimate sympathy with his readers. Engaged in ongoing conversations about themselves and their everyday world of gossip and news, literature and the theater, courtship and marriage, personalities and social events, readers are eagerly drawn into accord with Bickerstaff's point of view and so with the standards of conduct and taste he promotes. Bickerstaff's self-mockery and his ironizing approach to the objects of his criticism, then, signal not the abandonment of didacticism, but rather a particularly shrewd rhetoric for its effective operation.

As self-designated "Censors" of Great Britain, the authors of *The Tatler* and *The Spectator* address their readers through pseudonymous personae. Steele borrowed the fictional persona of Isaac Bickerstaff from Jonathan Swift, author of *Gulliver's Travels.* In February 1708, Swift had popularized Bickerstaff in a satiric tract called *Predictions for the Year 1708.* Bickerstaff, an astrologer, was a send-up of an actual quack astrologer, John Partridge, who had published a series of preposterous prophecies in his almanacs (an exception to Addison's rule of not naming names). In *Predictions for the Year 1708*, Bickerstaff predicts that Partridge will die of a fever at eleven o'clock on the night of March 29 (Swift, *Bickerstaff Papers* 145). The joke and the fictional Bickerstaff take on a life of their own in a series of pamphlets.

Apparently, the victim of this ruse didn't fully get it. In his 1709 almanac, Partridge confidently declares that he is, in fact, still alive and so living proof of the invalidity of Bickerstaff's "prediction" of his death. In the first number of *The Tatler*, Steele's Bickerstaff contradicts Partridge's claim and reasserts the accuracy of his prediction. He is speaking figuratively of those intellectual and moral "deaths" he will take as his satiric objects in *The Tatler*:

> . . . there is an *Almanack* come out for the Year 1709. In one Page of which, it is asserted by the said *John Partridge*, That he is still living. . . . I have . . . sufficiently convinc'd this Man that he is dead, and if he has any Shame, I don't doubt but that by this Time he owns it to all his Acquaintance: For tho' the Legs and Arms, and whole Body, of that Man may still appear and perform their animal Functions; yet since, as I have elsewhere observ'd, his Art is gone, the Man is gone. . . . I shall, as I see Occasion, proceed to confute other dead Men, who pretend to be in Being, that they are actually deceased. (see p. 54)

The conceit continues in *Tatler* No. 99, which announces Partridge's "burial." In *Tatler* No. 110, Bickerstaff persists in his satiric project, presiding as Chief Justice over a "Court of Honor" in order to convict those men and women who, though alive in body, are, like Partridge, "dead in Reason" (see p. 478).

By adopting the persona of Isaac Bickerstaff, Steele ties his paper to a well-known, if fictional, personality. Entertained by the running joke against Partridge for a year, readers are familiar with Bickerstaff and know him as an agent of witty satire. Steele's importation of Bickerstaff sets a playful, ironic tone, but it also establishes a central, unifying voice through which the widely various subject matter of *The Tatler* can be focused and controlled.

Although in its earlier numbers *The Tatler* contained a good deal of foreign and domestic political views, such reporting became rarer as the paper came to rely ever more heavily on its moral and critical essays. Yet *The Tatler* never entirely abandoned its news reporting or its outspoken political engagements. And its demise seems tied to a set of political entanglements in Steele's career. While it is not perfectly certain why Steele stopped publication in January 1711, he seems to have acted in response to the ascension of a new Tory ministry under Harley. Writing behind the mask of Isaac Bickerstaff, Steele's authorship of *The Tatler* was an open secret, but his paper's pro-Whig political stance was no secret at all.

During the previous fall, Steele held three professional positions: as Isaac Bickerstaff, editor of *The Tatler;* editor of the *Gazette,* the official newspaper of the government; and commissioner for stamp duties. In October 1710, apparently as part of the change in the ministry and its bureaucracy, he lost his position as gazetteer but not his appointment as commissioner. There is evidence that Steele made some sort of deal with the new ministry, agreeing to cease publication of *The Tatler* in return for the continuance of his commissionership, a post worth £300 a year.

Only two months after the end of *The Tatler,* however, Steele jumped back into the periodical enterprise, by starting up *The Spectator* in a joint venture with his friend Addison. The first number appeared on March 1, 1711, written in the guise of a new persona, Mr. Spectator. While retaining much of the self-mocking, ironizing rhetoric of Isaac Bickerstaff, Mr. Spectator puts himself at greater distance not only from his audience but from the very world in which he lives. This gentleman lives quietly, at a certain remove from "the World, rather as a Spectator of Mankind, than as one of the Species" (*Spectator* No. 1). He constructs an image of himself as a detached, quasi-invisible character, with no self-identifying attachment to any scene of life, be it business, the theater, the country, the city, the coffeehouse, or the private home.

He introduces himself in the first number of *The Spectator* by throwing a veil of secrecy around all those identifying features of body, dress, and complexion, and all those indexes of name, age, and address that would locate him in, rather than apart from, the world. Withholding his own identity, he tends, chameleonlike, to take on that of whatever company he finds himself in: "I have been taken for a Merchant upon the *Exchange* for above these ten Years, and sometimes pass for a *Jew* in the Assembly of Stock-Jobbers at *Jonathan's*" (*Spectator* No. 1; see p. 81). Anonymous, he can move with equal ease, as a kind of invisible eye, through all scenes of life. His profession as spectator, then, does not involve him in any arena of enterprise, but rather in observing and evaluating those who do participate from a position outside, if not above, their world. Mr. Spectator's invisibility is a cultivated aspect of his character on which the ethos and perspective of the paper depend. It is a necessary condition of his superior insight into the affairs and character of humankind. He can, then, "discern the Errors in the Oeconomy, Business, and Diversion of others, better than those who are engaged in them" (*Spectator* No. 1; see p. 81). "The inward Disposition of the Mind" is "made visible" to his veiled surveillance (*Spectator* No. 86).

Often ironic, such critical detachment provides him with a "better Perspective" on the world even as it also protects him from the world. While he can see and fully identify others — their foibles and virtues, their motivations and goals — he does all he can to make sure that others cannot recognize and identify him. His projects depend on this immunity so completely that his greatest fear is having his cover blown, of becoming visible: "the greatest Pain I can suffer, is . . . being talked to, and being stared at" (*Spectator* No. 1; see p. 82). Once *seen*, the Spectator would become the object of another's gaze and, potentially, of another's evaluation, another's criticism. The authority of his observations seems to depend on his own immunity from the critical observation of others.

Always the observer and never the observed, unattached, and apparently dispassionate, Mr. Spectator is an early embodiment of what becomes the type of the modern critic. The validity of his criticism rests on the (alleged) absence of personal interest, on its impersonality and objectivity. The criteria according to which the Spectator's criticism operates are not presented as those of an individual man looking out for his own interests and concerns, but as those of an impersonal arbiter of the "higher," more absolute standards of nature, law, civilization, and humanity itself.

COMMERCE, TASTE, AND CULTURE

The critical stance of *The Tatler* and *The Spectator* is in good part determined by their position in an increasingly commercialized British society. Colonial expansion, as well as financial, commercial, and technical innovation, was providing more things at better prices to greater numbers of people. Mass commercial consumption and mass culture are products of the fully industrialized nineteenth century, but the blueprint for a recognizably modern consumer society was being drawn up in the eighteenth.

Eighteenth-century cultural commentators remark again and again, with dismay, amusement, and scorn, on their contemporaries' obsession with getting and spending. *The Tatler* and *The Spectator* paint a picture of a society in which almost all social practices and institutions are colored and shaped (often to their detriment) by commercial, rather than more purely ethical, values. These papers are anxious to separate the faulty values that drive commerce — self-interest, novelty and impermanence, profit and loss — from their own stabilizing ethic of rational benevolence, community, and common sense. This ethic is promoted as an antidote to the selfishness, the superficiality, the ephemerality, the frippery, and the foolishness of modern life.

We find here an outline of what has become a commonplace opposition between, on the one hand, a commercialized realm of superficial and ephemeral vanity — the home of get-rich-quick schemes, of fashion, novelty, ostentation, and materialism — and, on the other, an ethical and aesthetic arena of internal and permanent value — the home of benevolence, good sense, and good taste, which offers an alternative to the commercial market. Of course, this set of ethical and aesthetic values is only figuratively a "place," yet it was meant to have very real effects on the actual content of minds and conduct of lives.

The Tatler and *The Spectator* are eager to establish a sphere of value and identification outside the commercial marketplace, where taste and culture are bought and sold with little regard to any standard higher than the latest fashion. As they conceptualize and represent this place, *The Tatler* and *The Spectator* go far in articulating the modern realm of culture: an aesthetic and ethical arena for the improvement of human nature responsive to criteria other than status, wealth, and fashionability, which mark the commercial ethic. As Leslie Stephen says of Addison: "He is a genuine prophet of what we now describe as Culture" (74).

This promised land of "Culture" of which Addison is the "prophet" has most commonly been associated with his realm of the imagination. In *Spectator* Nos. 411–21 Addison provides a kind of blueprint for the operation of the mental and affective faculties associated with what we now call aesthetic pleasure (see pp. 387–96). These pleasures, like Mr. Spectator's own most characteristic faculty, are visual; the pleasures of the imagination are first the pleasures of looking, either literally or imaginatively. Addison's imaginative vision and its pleasures stand as a kind of superior alternative to the pleasures of material acquisition they so closely mirror. The "Man of a Polite Imagination," Addison proposes in *Spectator* No. 411, "often feels a greater Satisfaction in the Prospect of Fields and Meadows, than another does in the Possession. It gives him, indeed, a kind of Property in every thing he sees" (see p. 388).

Here we can see how the principles of access and privilege that govern the bourgeois public sphere overlap with those of the aesthetic realm of the imagination. Wealth and status are immaterial in truly rational and polite discourse. All one needs is a commitment to a shared standard of universal human reason. Similarly, the aesthetic pleasures are not only independent, they are superior to the satisfactions of material wealth and ownership. If the imagination functions as a superior kind of "ownership," it also functions as a kind of purely cognitive colonization. It roams, bringing "into our reach some of the most remote Parts of the Universe" (No. 411; see p. 387). The terms Addison uses show the imagination as a mental way of grasping and possessing, as much a reflection of, as an alternative to, the mundane world of getting and spending.

The emergence of modern categories of culture and taste occurs alongside the commercial saturation of everyday London life. In relation to the development of ideas about the cultural aesthetic, the commercialization of literature (with its attendant commodification of knowledge) and of entertainment and leisure are the most relevant. The eighteenth-century man or woman about town could choose from a growing variety of public and commercial forms of entertainment and "culture": plays, operas, acrobatics, puppet shows, waxwork shows, masquerades, pleasure gardens, collections of curious and novel things in museums, public houses, and retail shops. This is the age of the first great entrepreneurs of leisure. But if anything that sells gets published or staged, then how can a standard of taste be maintained? The answer lies in the power of choice exercised by those who buy. Clearly, this audience must be educated to choose what is tasteful and correct.

Chronology
of the Lives and Times
of Addison and Steele

1672

March 12: Richard Steele born in Dublin.

May 1: Joseph Addison born in Wiltshire.

1684

Steele enters Charterhouse School in London, where he remains until 1689.

1685

Charles II dies; James II takes throne.

1686

Addison enters Charterhouse, where he becomes Steele's friend and remains until 1687.

1687

Addison enters Queen's and Magdalen colleges at Oxford. He completes his undergraduate career in 1691.

1688–89

The Glorious Revolution: James flees to France; William of Orange arrives in England.

1689

Steele enters Christ Church and Merton colleges at Oxford, where he remains until 1694.

William III and Mary II (James II's daughter) ascend throne.

1691

Addison becomes a tutor at Oxford.

1693

Addison receives his M.A.

1694

Addison contributes poems to Jacob Tonson's *Miscellanies*. Bank of England instituted. Mary II dies.

1694–95

Steele leaves Oxford without a degree and joins the Horse Guards.

1695–1700

Steele becomes ensign and then captain in the Coldstream Guards.

1698

Addison becomes a fellow of Magdalen College.

1699–1704

Addison travels and studies in France, Italy, Switzerland, Austria, Germany, and Holland.

1702

England joins in the War of the Spanish Succession. William II dies; Anne becomes Queen of England.

1704

Addison returns to England and publishes *The Campaign*, a poem celebrating Marlborough's victory at Blenheim.

1705

Addison appointed undersecretary of state and publishes his *Remarks on Italy*. Steele's *The Tender Husband* produced. Steele marries Margaret Stretch.

1706

As undersecretary of state, Addison goes on a diplomatic mission to the Court of Hanover with Lord Halifax. Steele appointed gentleman waiter to Prince George of Denmark, husband of Queen Anne. Steele's wife dies.

Act of Union unites England and Scotland as Great Britain.

1707

March: Addison's opera *Rosamond* performed. Steele appointed gazetteer through the influence of Arthur Maynwaring. Steele marries Mary Scurlock.

1708

Addison appointed secretary to Lord Wharton, the new lord-lieutenant of Ireland. Addison elected M.P. for Lostwithiel. Swift publishes Bickerstaff pamphlets.

1709

April 12: Steele begins *The Tatler*.

Addison in Dublin with Lord-Lieutenant Wharton (until 1710).

1710

October: Steele made a commissioner of the Stamp Office and loses his position as gazetteer with the fall of the Whig government.

Addison elected M.P. for Malmesbury.

1711

January 2: *The Tatler* ends.

March 1: Addison and Steele begin *The Spectator*.

1712

December 6: *The Spectator* ends.

1713

March: Addison's *Cato* produced.

Steele publishes *The Guardian* from March 12 to October 1, and *The Englishman* from October 6, 1713, to February 14, 1714. Steele elected M.P. for Stockbridge.

Peace of Utrecht negotiated between England and France, ending the War of the Spanish Succession.

1714

With Eustace Budgell and Thomas Tickell, Addison begins second series of *The Spectator,* which runs from June 18 until December 20. Steele publishes anti-Tory political pamphlets, including *The Crisis,* and is expelled from Parliament for these attacks. In August and

September, after the death of Queen Anne, the Whig government comes back into power. Addison appointed secretary to the Regency and to the Lords Justices. Steele becomes manager of Drury Lane Theatre. Addison reappointed to his position as secretary to the lord-lieutenant of Ireland.

Queen Anne dies; George I takes throne. Robert Walpole appointed prime minister.

1715

Addison appointed a commissioner of trade. Addison writes *The Freeholder,* which runs from December 13, 1715, until June 25, 1716. Steele elected M.P. for Boroughbridge and is knighted by George I. Steele revives *The Englishman;* it runs from July 11 until November 21.

1716

March: Addison's comedy *The Drummer* produced.

Addison marries the Countess of Warwick. Steele publishes *Town Talk* from December 17, 1715, until February 15, 1716. As commissioner of trade, Steele visits Scotland.

1717

Addison made secretary of state. Steele makes another visit to Scotland. Steele's wife dies.

1718

Because of poor health, Addison resigns as secretary of state.

1719

January 30: Addison's daughter, Charlotte, born.

June 17: Addison dies.

1720

Steele engages in a controversy with the Duke of Newcastle over the management of the Drury Lane Theatre. Newcastle terminates his post there.

South Sea investment venture collapses ("South Sea Bubble").

1721

Steele returns to managership at the Drury Lane Theatre.

1722

November: Steele's *The Conscious Lovers* performed.

Steele elected M.P. for Wendover.

1726
Steele partially paralyzed by a stroke.

1727
George I dies; George II takes throne.

1729
September 1: Steele dies.

A Note on the Text

The papers from *The Tatler* and *The Spectator* have been reprinted from Donald F. Bond's invaluable Oxford editions, published by the Clarendon Press. I am indebted to Bond's scholarship for some of the notes I have included with my own. Where I have used Bond's information, I credit it thus: [Bond]. Many thanks to Oxford University Press for their permission to reproduce these papers.

For ease of reference, I have provided an editorial title in brackets at the start of every paper. The title gives credit to the individual paper's author, except in cases where authorship is undetermined.

Wherever possible, the text of the documents in the "Cultural Contexts" that accompany the papers in each of the four chapters is that of the original edition or of the most authoritative edition. Unless otherwise indicated in the document headnote, the text used is that of the original edition. Original spelling and punctuation have been retained in the documents, although the long *s* has been modernized.

The SPECTATOR.

Non fumum ex fulgore, fed ex fumo dare lucem
Cogitat, ut fpeciofa dehinc miracula promat. Hor.

To be Continued every Day.

Thurfday, March 1. 1711.

I Have obferved, that a Reader feldom perufes a Book with Pleafure 'till he knows whether the Writer of it be a black or a fair Man, of a mild or cholerick Difpofition, Married or a Batchelor, with other Particulars of the like nature, that conduce very much to the right Underftanding of an Author. To gratify this Curiofity, which is fo natural to a Reader, I defign this Paper, and my next, as Prefatory Difcourfes to my following Writing, and fhall give fome Account in them of the fevral Perfons that are engaged in this Work. As the chief Trouble of Compiling, Digefting and Correcting will fall to my Share, I muft do my felf the Juftice to open the Work with my own Hiftory.

I was born to a fmall Hereditary Eftate, which I find, by the Writings of the Family, was bounded by the fame Hedge and Ditches in *William* the Conqueror's Time that it is at prefent, and has been delivered down from Father to Son whole and entire, without the Lofs or Acquifition of a fingle Field or Meadow, during the Space of fix hundred Years. There goes a Story in the Family, that when my Mother was gone with Child of me about three Months, fhe dreamt that fhe was brought to Bed of a Judge: Whether this might proceed from a Law-Suit which was then depending in the Family, or my Father's being a Juftice of th. Peace, I cannot determine; for I am not fo vain as to think it prefaged any Dignity that I fhould arrive at in my futur Life, though that was the Interpretation which the Neighbourhood put upon it. The Gravity of my Behaviour at my very firft Appearance in the Weld, and all the Time that I fucked, feemed to favour my Mother's Dream: For, as fhe has often told me, I threw away my Rattle before I was two Months old, and would not make ufe of my Coral 'till they had taken away the Bells from it

As for the reft of my Infancy, there being nothing in it remarkable, I fhall pafs it over in Silence. I find, that, during my Nonage, I had the Reputation of a very fullen Youth, but was always a Favourite of my School-Mafter, who ufed to fay, *that my Parts were folid and would wear well*. I had not been long at the Univerfity, before I di-

ftinguifhed my felf by a moft profound Silence: For, during the Space of eight Years, excepting in the publick Exercifes of the College, I fcarce uttered the Quantity of an hundred Words; and indeed do not remember that I ever fpoke three Sentences together in my whole Life. Whilft I was in this Learned Body I applied my felf with fo much Diligence to my Studies, that there are very few celebrated Books, either in the Learned or the Modern Tongues, which I am not acquainted with.

Upon the Death of my Father I was refolved to travel into Foreign Countries, and therefore left the Univerfity, with the Character of an odd unaccountable Fellow, that had a great deal of Learning, if I would but fhow it. An infatiable Thirft after Knowledge carried me into all the Countries of *Europe*, where there was any thing new or ftrange to be feen; nay, to fuch a Degree was my Curiofity raifed, that having read the Controverfies of fome great Men concerning the Antiquities of *Egypt*, I made a Voyage to *Grand Cairo*, on purpofe to take the Meafure of a Pyramid; and as foon as I had fet my felf right in that Particular, returned to my Native Country with great Satisfaction.

I have paffed my latter Years in this City, where I am frequently feen in moft publick Places, tho' there are not above half a dozen of my felect Friends that know me; of whom my next Paper fhall give a more particular Account. There is no Place of publick Refort, wherein I do not often make my Appearance; fometimes I am feen thrufting my Head into a Round of Politicians at *Will's*, and liftning with great Attention to the Narratives that are made in thofe little Circular Audiences. Sometimes I fmoak a Pipe at *Child's*; and whilft I feem attentive to nothing but the *Poft-Man*, over-hear the Converfation of every Table in the Room. I appear on *Sunday* Nights at St. *James's* Coffee-Houfe, and fometimes join the little Committee of Politicks in the Inner-Room, as one who comes there to hear and improve. My Face is likewife very well known at the *Grecian*, the *Cocoa-Tree*, and in the Theaters both of *Drury-Lane*, and the *Hay-Market*. I have been taken for a Merchant upon

---

First page of *The Spectator* No. 1 (Thursday, March 1, 1711).

Periodical Papers and
the Market of Public Opinion

The selections from *The Tatler* and *The Spectator* included here focus on their place in the booming market of periodical publications. Both papers engage in an ongoing process of self-definition that often emphasizes their difference from other periodicals, such as the *Gazette*, which were completely devoted to news of current events, and Defoe's *Review*, which were mostly political and polemic. In *Tatler* No. 178, Isaac Bickerstaff offers his paper as a periodical antidote to news addiction, and in *Spectator* No. 262, Mr. Spectator declares, "my Paper has not in it a single Word of News." The papers distinguish themselves as well from sensationalist journals, those slanderous sheets of early yellow journalism beloved by readers like the correspondent who complains to *The Female Tatler* that it has too little scandal (see No. 98, p. 133).

But *The Tatler* and *The Spectator* also bear a positive relation to their competitors. *The Tatler*, as evidenced by the full first number, did contain news of current events and so was to some extent a newspaper like many others. Few elements in *The Tatler* and *The Spectator* had not appeared already in earlier periodicals. The device of the fictional Spectator Club, for example, follows Defoe's Scandalous Club, which he used as a forum for exposing vice and folly (see p. 122). Like Defoe, Addison and Steele scrupulously claim to be free of personal references and libelous scandalmongering. Their great popularity depends on a careful balancing of the familiar and the novel. Among other similarities, *The Tatler* and *The Spectator* look *like* every other periodical and newspaper of the day. So while they often insist on the *differences* between their own and other periodicals, they rely upon a market and a form that were well established, if not fully mined.

Once they appear, *The Tatler* and *The Spectator* inspire a submarket of imitators and must then differentiate themselves from these "numberless Vermin that feed upon this Paper" (*Tatler* No. 229; see p. 74). Imitation is, of course, a high form of flattery, and as John Gay notes in "The Present State of Wit," *The Tatler* was by far the most popular periodical to date. Those "whole Swarms of little Satyrical" imitators were simply trying to get in on a sure thing (see p. 154). After *The Spectator* ceased publication, both Steele and Addison went on to author other periodical papers, like those from *The Guardian* collected here (see p. 156). All these texts vied in a competitive market where *The Tatler* and *The Spectator* constantly asserted their distinctive superiority to keep their market advantage.

More important than the imitation they inspired among writers was the ethical emulation the papers aroused in their readers. By claiming to be free of party politics and unconcerned with the news, these papers define their mission as ethical and social, rather than political or journalistic. This focus on social reform is typical of their age: the contextual materials included here attest to the drive for reform of manners and morals in early eighteenth-century England.

The Tatler and *The Spectator* also distinguish their approach to reform from that of illiberal institutions like the Society for the Reformation of Manners and Morals. In the passage from Josiah Woodward's *Account of the Societies for Reformation of Manners*, we can mark these differences (see p. 115). The Society is zealous and puritanical, the papers casual and benevolent. The Society is concerned largely with vice and sin, the papers with folly and affectation. The Society targets the "mob" of common people, the papers the bourgeois professional classes and the fashionable elite. The Society strives to ferret out, by whatever means, and persecute sinfully vicious individuals; it operates through formal legal enforcement. An appendix to Woodward's volume (not collected here) contains an abstract of all the statutes against Sabbath breaking, swearing, prostitution, and public drunkenness, currently on the books.

In contrast, the reformative campaigns waged through *The Tatler* and *The Spectator* deploy those informal, persuasive modes of power that characterize the bourgeois public sphere and liberal hegemonic power more generally. The identities of Isaac Bickerstaff and Mr. Spectator are defined by their extralegislative social roles. As Bickerstaff says, "the greatest Evils in Human Society are such that no Law can come at" (*Tatler* No. 61). Addison and Steele operate under the assumption that in order to truly reform what people do, one must not lock them up but change how they think. In the first number of *The Tatler*, Steele puts it in no uncertain terms: "It is both a Charitable and Necessary Work to offer something, whereby such worthy and well-affected Members of the Commonwealth may be instructed, after their Reading, *what to think*" (see p. 49). Along with all their competitors, then, the papers strive for prominence in an ongoing contest for influence over public opinion.

The period under examination is conventionally dubbed the Age of Satire, and the satire is above all social satire, a form of sociocultural criticism. Eighteenth-century authors exposed the follies and vices of their contemporaries, not purely to entertain, but also to educate their audience. Almost all the collateral texts embody this satiric force in a range of satiric rhetorics and perspectives, demonstrating that stylistic differences may signal substantial divergences in ideology and general worldview. Compared to the writing of their contemporaries, figures like Edward Ward and Daniel Defoe, *The Tatler* and *The Spectator* share a studied, critical attention to the forms and impulses of London life. Yet they embody and promote an ideal of optimism and refinement often absent from the harsh, deeply pessimistic satiric vision exemplified by Edward Ward.

The gentility and subtlety of Bickerstaff and Mr. Spectator may best be appreciated by comparing them with Ward's *The London Spy*, a much "lower," and certainly more reactionary, view of London life. Ward's London coffeehouses are the same ones Addison and Steele visit and describe, yet they seem to belong to another universe: they are painted as dens of iniquity, chaotic Pandemoniums peopled by grotesques, the smoky pens of the nearly insane and deluded. Ward's dark vision has more in common with *The Character of a Coffee-House* (1673) than with *The Tatler* and *The Spectator* (see p. 137).

The satire of Addison and Steele reduces to harmonious order the rambling, rough-and-tumble chaos of Ward's London. Perceiving its objects more selectively and placing them under a sunnier light, it establishes a calmer, less frenetic world, one constructed not from the jarring contrasts and heaped-up similes that mark Ward's rhetoric, but from balanced syntactical symmetries and carefully controlled figurative language. The grotesque is refined away. The world of *The Tatler* and *The Spectator* is a place of folly, and even vice; yet this world is human and urbane, not monstrous. The papers probe human nature not to reveal its bedrock depravity but to expose a common core of reason, sense, and sentiment.

The controlled unity and studied development achieved in the best of *The Tatler* and *The Spectator* papers become more apparent when they are viewed against the foil of the often hastily written, fragmented, and somewhat underdeveloped papers in *The Female Tatler*. This spin-off shares much of the genteel bourgeois ideology of *The Tatler* but lacks its polish and sustained attention. In addition, while the number of topical references in *The Tatler* and *The Spectator* seem daunting at first, in comparison with other papers, like Defoe's *Review*, they are relatively accessible, even to twentieth-century readers. To a greater degree than most contemporaneous publications, whose vision often seems to extend no further than the horizon of the next day, *The Tatler* and *The Spectator* look for a more permanent place in the history of letters. Addison and Steele self-consciously strive to temper the generic ephemerality of the papers by publishing them in bound volumes and by making the local and particular context of their meditations yield observations understood as eternal and universally human. The long-lived accessibility of *The Tatler* and *The Spectator* was consciously built into their plan, especially in the case of the latter, which completely detached itself from news coverage. As we see in *Spectator* No. 435, in chronicling contemporary manners and mores, the papers strive to generalize beyond the purely topical and occasional, to address topics of enduring concern (see p. 539). Such efforts to define and address a "universal" audience marks *The Tatler* and *The Spectator* as pioneering agents of the bourgeois public sphere. They reflect the ideals of rationality, common sense, public access, plain English, and universal humanity that characterize the liberal ideology of the emerging public sphere.

These ideals also characterize the vigorous coffeehouse culture that sprang up in London in the late seventeenth and early eighteenth centuries. The intimate affiliation between the commercial periodical press and coffeehouse society establishes a closed circuit of production and consumption. Presumably written, and even generated in the discussions at particular coffeehouses, each section in *The Tatler* is in turn circulated and read in the coffeehouses, refueling the conversation.

Coffeehouse society and *The Tatler* and *The Specator* are alike in their inclusivity, in the sheer range of human pursuits and types they encompass. *The Character of a Coffee-House*, a satiric pamphlet, emphasizes the social promiscuity that marks coffeehouse society (see p. 137). The coffeehouse, like Noah's Ark, "receives Animals of every sort" and serves as a forum for discussions and pursuits that are as varied as its clientele. It is an arena for gossip, for scientific conversation, for legal, political, religious, and literary criticism. Most important, at the coffeehouse every man can take up the mantle of statesman, politician, and critic. The coffeehouse is "a *High-Court of Justice*, where every little fellow . . . takes upon him to transpose Affairs both in Church and State, to shew reasons against *Acts* of Parliament, and condemn the Decrees of *general Councels*" (see *The Character of a Coffee-House*, p. 137).

All these aspects of coffeehouse culture are reflected in *The Tatler* and *The Spectator*. But while *The Character* speaks of the coffeehouse with scorn and derision, Addison and Steele more often celebrate, indeed exploit, the relaxing of status distinctions, the range of functions, and the freedom of conversation. The coffeehouse clientele is the core of their audience. Bickerstaff and Mr. Spectator take on the judicial prescription of manners and mores, establishing each paper as precisely that sort of "High Court of Justice" that figures the coffeehouse in the earlier pamphlet. As in the coffeehouses, the whole compass of human endeavor and experience is embraced in the pages of *The Tatler* and *The Spectator*. The sheer range of the papers' topics may be quickly gleaned from *Spectator* No. 46, where Mr. Spectator's notes for various papers are discovered before a coffeehouse audience.

Eager to claim a similar breadth of audience and range of influence, Mrs. Crackenthorpe, the narrating persona of *The Female Tatler*, likewise orients her paper toward London's coffeehouse and club society. But this alignment must be indirect, for, as a woman, Mrs. Crackenthorpe is excluded from coffeehouses. Since she can't go to the coffeehouses, she brings them, or at least their clientele and conversations, into her drawing room: "I shall date all my advices from my own apartment, which comprehends, White's, Will's, the Grecian, Garraway's, in Exchange Alley," "since grave statesmen, airy beaus, lawyers, cits, poets and parsons, and ladies of all degrees assemble there" (*Female Tatler* No. 1; see p. 131).

In these texts, we see a drive toward a totally comprehensive account of contemporary life and manners, one that strives to bring all the world under its umbrella of reform. But as we may note in Mrs. Crackenthorpe's outline for her paper, such comprehensiveness demands a survey that goes beyond exclusively male arenas like coffeehouses, the courts, and the stock exchange to encompass the realm of feminine domesticity. A full account of the world must include drawing rooms filled with "ladies of all degrees" just as surely as it includes coffeehouses filled with gentlemen of all degrees. *The Tatler* and *The Spectator* likewise address both ladies and gentlemen, encompassing private and public arenas of experience. In the inaugural issue of *The Tatler*, Steele announces: "I resolve also to have something which may be of Entertainment to the Fair Sex, in Honour of whom I have invented the Title of this Paper" (see pp. 49–50). Moving between the masculine and feminine spheres of experience, *The Tatler* and *The Spectator* define them in ways that are at once discriminatory and integrative. As selections in Chapter 4 show, Addison and Steele emphatically advocate the gendered separation of spheres: the domestic arena is proper to women; the public, commercial, and political arena, to men. Yet in the papers themselves these two spheres meet and combine in ways meant to integrate them as complements to one another. *The Tatler* and *The Spectator* provide crucial data for our historical understanding of the modern gendered separation of spheres and of the ways in which these "separate" spheres are actually highly interdependent and interconnected.

The Tatler

Dedication to Mr. Maynwaring[1]
[Steele on the Purpose of the Paper]

SIR,

The State of Conversation and Business in this Town having been long perplexed with Pretenders in both Kinds, in order to open Men's Eyes against such Abuses, it appeared no unprofitable Undertaking to publish a Paper which should observe upon the Manners of the Pleasurable, as well as the Busie Part of Mankind. To make this generally read, it seemed the most proper Method to form it by Way of a Letter of Intelligence, consisting of such Parts as might gratify the Curiosity of Persons of all Conditions, and of each Sex. But a Work of this Nature requiring Time to grow into the Notice of the World, it happened very luckily, that a little before I had resolved upon this Design, a Gentleman[2] had written Predictions, and Two or Three other Pieces in my Name, which had rendered it famous thro' all Parts of *Europe*; and by an inimitable Spirit and Humour, raised it to as high a Pitch of Reputation as it could possibly arrive at.

By this good Fortune, the Name of *Isaac Bickerstaff* gained an Audience of all who had any Taste of Wit, and the Addition or the ordinary Occurrences of common Journals of News brought in a Multitude of other Readers. I could not, I confess, long keep up the Opinion of the Town, that these Lucubrations were written by the same Hand with the first Works which were published under my Name; but before I lost the Participation of that Author's Fame, I had already found the Advantage of his Authority, to which I owe the sudden Acceptance which my Labours met with in the World.

The general Purpose of this Paper, is to expose the false Arts of Life, to pull off the Disguises of Cunning, Vanity, and Affectation, and to recommend a general Simplicity in our Dress, our Discourse, and our Behaviour. No Man has a better Judgment for the Discovery, or a nobler Spirit for the Contempt of all Imposture, than your self; which Qualities render you the most proper Patron for the Author of

---

[1] *Maynwaring:* Arthur Maynwaring (1688–1712) was a prominent Whig journalist and a close associate of Addison, and more especially of Steele. Against the Tory *Examiner* he wrote the Whig paper *The Medley*, to which Steele contributed.

[2] *a Gentleman:* This is a reference to Jonathan Swift's Bickerstaff writings against Partridge. See the Introduction (pp. 27–28).

The TATLER.

By *Isaac Bickerstaff* Esq;

Quicquid agunt Homines nostri Farrago Libelli.

Tuesday, April 12. 1709.

THO' *the other Papers which are publish'd for the Use of the good People of* England *have certainly very wholesome Effects, and are laudable in their particular Kinds, they do not seem to come up to the main Design of such Narrations, which, I humbly presume, should be principally intended for the Use of Politick Persons, who are so publick-spirited as to neglect their own Affairs to look into Transactions of State. Now these Gentlemen, for the most Part, being Persons of strong Zeal and weak Intellects, it is both a Charitable and Necessary Work to offer something, whereby such worthy and well-affected Members of the Commonwealth may be instructed, after their Reading, what to think: Which shall be the End and Purpose of this my Paper, wherein I shall from Time to Time Report and Consider all Matters of what Kind soever that shall occur to Me, and publish such my Advices and Reflections every* Tuesday, Thursday, *and* Saturday, *in the Week, for the Convenience of the Post. It is also resolv'd by me to have something which may be of Entertainment to the Fair Sex, in Honour of whom I have taken the Title of this Paper. I therefore earnestly desire all Persons, without Distinction, to take it in for the present Gratis, and hereafter at the Price of one Penny, forbidding all Hawkers to take more for it at their Peril. And I desire all Persons to consider, that I am at a very great Charge for proper Materials for this Work, as well as that before I resolv'd upon it, I had settled a Correspondence in all Parts of the Known and Knowing World; and forasmuch as this Globe is not trodden upon by mere Drudges of Business only, but that Men of Spirit and Genius are justly to be esteem'd as considerable Agents in it, we shall not upon a Dearth of News present you with musty Foreign Edicts, or dull Proclamations, but shall divide our Relation of the Passages which occur in Action or Discourse throughout this Town, as well as elsewhere, under such Dates of Places as may prepare you for the Matter you are to expect, in the following Manner.*

All Accounts of Gallantry, Pleasure, and Entertainment, shall be under the Article of White's *Chocolate-house; Poetry, under that of* Will's *Coffee-house; Learning, under the Title of* Grecian; *Foreign and Domestick News, you will have from* St. James's *Coffee-house; and what else I shall on any other Subject offer, shall be dated from my own Apartment.*

I once more desire my Reader to consider, That as I cannot keep an Ingenious Man to go daily to Will's, *under Twopence each Day merely for his Charges; to* White's, *under Sixpence; nor to the* Grecian, *without allowing him some Plain* Spanish, *to be at able at the Learned Table; and that a good Observer cannot speak with even Kidney at* St. James's *without some Linnen. I say, these Considerations will, I hope, make all Persons willing to comply with my Humble Request (when my Gratis Stock is exhausted) of a Penny a Piece; especially since they are sure of some Proper Amusement, and that it is impossible for me to want Means to entertain 'em, having, besides the Helps of my own Parts, the Power of Divination, and that I can, by casting a Figure, tell you all that will happen before it comes to pass.*

But this last Faculty I shall use very sparingly, and not speak of any Thing 'till it is pass'd, for fear of divulging Matters which may offend our Superiors.

White's Chocolate-House, April 7.

THE deplorable Condition of a very pretty Gentleman, who walks here at the Hours when Men of Quality first appear, is what is very much lamented. His History is, That on the 9th of *September*, 1705, being in his One and twentieth Year, he was washing his Teeth at a Tavern Window in *Pall-Mall*, when a fine Equipage pass'd by, and in it a young Lady who look'd up at him; away goes the Coach, and the young Gentleman pull'd off his Night-Cap, and instead of rubbing his Gums, as he ought to do, out of the Window 'till about Four a Clock, he sits him down, and spoke not a Word 'till Twelve at Night; after which, he began to enquire, if any Body knew the Lady ... The Company ask'd, What Lady? But he said no more, 'till they broke up at Six in the Morning. All the ensuing Winter he went from Church to Church every Sunday, and from Playhouse to Play-house all the Week, but could never find the Original of the Picture which dwelt in his Bosom. In a Word, his Attention to any Thing, but his Passion, was utterly gone. He has lost all the Money he ever play'd for, and been consulted in every Argument he has enter'd upon since the Moment he first saw her. He is of a Noble Family, has naturally a very good Air, is of a frank, honest Temper: But this Passion has so extreamly maul'd him, that his Features are set and uninform'd, and his whole Visage is deaden'd by a long Absence of Thought. He never appears in any Alacrity, but when rais'd by Wine; at which Time he is sure to come hither, and throw away a great deal of Wit on Fellows, who have no Sense further than just to observe, That our poor Lover has most Understanding

---

First page of *The Tatler* No. 1 (Tuesday, April 12, 1709).

these Essays. In the general, the Design, however executed, has met with so great Success, that there is hardly a Name now eminent among us for Power, Wit, Beauty, Valour, or Wisdom, which is not subscribed, for the Encouragement of these Volumes.[3] This is indeed an Honour, for which it is impossible to express a suitable Gratitude; and there is nothing could be an Addition to the Pleasure I take in it, but the Reflection that it gives me the most conspicuous Occasion I can ever have, of subscribing myself,

SIR,

Your most Obliged, most Obedient,

and most Humble Servant,

Isaac Bickerstaff.

No. 1
Tuesday, April 12, 1709
[Steele on Coffeehouses and The Tatler*]*

Quicquid agunt Homines nostri Farrago Libelli.[1]

Tho' the other Papers which are publish'd for the Use of the Good People of England *have certainly very wholesome Effects, and are laudable in their Particular Kinds, they do not seem to come up to the Main Design of such Narrations, which, I humbly presume, should be principally intended for the Use of Politick Persons, who are so publick-spirited as to neglect their own Affairs to look into Transactions of State. Now these Gentlemen, for the most Part, being Persons of strong Zeal and weak Intellects, it is both a Charitable and Necessary Work to offer something, whereby such worthy and well-affected Members of the Commonwealth may be instructed, after their Reading,* what to think: *Which shall be the End and Purpose of this my Paper, wherein I shall from Time to Time Report and Consider all Matters of what Kind soever that shall occur to Me, and publish such my Advices and Reflections every* Tuesday, Thursday, *and* Saturday, *in the Week, for the Convenience of the Post. I resolve also to have something which may be of Entertainment to the Fair*

---

[3] *these Volumes:* This dedication was included in a collected edition of *The Tatler* in four volumes, which appeared on July 10, 1710.

[1] *Quicquid . . . Libelli:* From Juvenal, *Satires* 1.85–86: "Whate'er men do, or say, or think, or dream, / Our motley paper seizes for its theme" — PERCY [Bond].

Sex, in Honour of whom I have invented the Title of this Paper. I therefore earnestly desire all Persons, without Distinction, to take it in for the present Gratis,[2] *and hereafter at the Price of One Penny, forbidding all Hawkers to take more for it at their Peril. And I desire all Persons to consider, that I am at a very great Charge for proper Materials for this Work, as well as that before I resolv'd upon it, I had settled a Correspondence in all Parts of the Known and Knowing World. And forasmuch as this Globe is not trodden upon by mere Drudges of Business only, but that Men of Spirit and Genius are justly to be esteem'd as considerable Agents in it, we shall not upon a Dearth of News present you with musty Foreign Edicts, or dull Proclamations, but shall divide our Relations of the Passages which occur in Action or Discourse throughout this Town, as well as else-where, under such Dates of Places as may prepare you for the Matter you are to expect, in the following Manner.*

All Accounts of Gallantry, Pleasure, *and* Entertainment, *shall be under the Article of* White's *Chocolate-house;* Poetry, *under that of* Will's *Coffee-house;* Learning, *under the Title of* Graecian; Foreign *and* Domestick News, *you will have from St.* James's *Coffee-house; and what else I have to offer on any other Subject, shall be dated from my own* Apartment.[3]

I once more desire my Reader to consider, That as I cannot keep an Ingenious Man to go daily to Will's, *under Twopence each Day merely for his Charges; to* White's, *under Sixpence; nor to the* Grae-cian, *without allowing him some Plain* Spanish,[4] *to be as able as oth-ers at the Learned Table; and that a good Observer cannot speak with even* Kidney[5] *at St.* James's *without clean Linnen. I say, these Considerations will, I hope, make all Persons willing to comply with my Humble Request (when my* Gratis *Stock is exhausted) of a Penny a Piece; especially since they are sure of some Proper Amusement, and that it is impossible for me to want Means to entertain 'em, hav-ing, besides the Force of my own Parts, the Power of Divination, and that I can, by casting a Figure, tell you all that will happen before it comes to pass.*

---

[2] *Gratis:* For free. The first four numbers of *The Tatler* were given out at no charge; after this they cost a penny.

[3] *All Accounts . . . Apartment:* Here Steele categorizes the subject matter of his pa-pers to correspond with the character of each of these prominent coffeehouses: White's was famous as the resort of men of fashion, and accounts of "Gallantry, Pleasure, and Entertainment" will be dated from it; Will's was known as the gathering place of liter-ary men, and essays on poetry will issue from there, and so on.

[4] *Plain Spanish:* Snuff, a tobacco product inhaled through the nose.

[5] *Kidney:* Humphrey Kidney was a waiter at St. James's Coffee-house.

But this last Faculty I shall use very sparingly, and speak but of few Things 'till they are pass'd, for fear of divulging Matters which may offend our Superiors.

White's Chocolate-house, April 7.

The deplorable Condition of a very pretty Gentleman, who walks here at the Hours when Men of Quality first appear, is what is very much lamented. His History is, That on the 9th of *September*, 1705, being in his One and twentieth Year, he was washing his Teeth at a Tavern Window in *Pall-Mall*,[6] when a fine Equipage pass'd by, and in it a young Lady who look'd up at him; away goes the Coach, and the young Gentleman pull'd off his Night-Cap, and instead of rubbing his Gums, as he ought to do, out of the Window 'till about Four of Clock, he sits him down, and spoke not a Word 'till Twelve at Night; after which, he began to enquire, If any body knew the Lady — The Company ask'd, What Lady? But he said no more, 'till they broke up at Six in the Morning. All the ensuing Winter he went from Church to Church every Sunday, and from Play-house to Play-house every Night in the Week, but could never find the Original of the Picture which dwelt in his Bosom. In a Word, his Attention to any Thing, but his Passion, was utterly gone. He has lost all the Money he ever play'd for, and been confuted in every Argument he has enter'd upon since the Moment he first saw her. He is of a Noble Family, has naturally a very good Air, is of a frank, honest Temper: But this Passion has so extremely maul'd him, that his Features are set and uninform'd, and his whole Visage is deaden'd by a long Absence of Thought. He never appears in any Alacrity, but when rais'd by Wine; at which Time he is sure to come hither, and throw away a great deal of Wit on Fellows, who have no Sense further than just to observe, That our poor Lover has most Understanding when he's Drunk, and is least in his Senses when he's Sober.

Will's Coffee-house, April 8.

On *Thursday* last was acted, for the Benefit of Mr. *Betterton*,[7] the Celebrated Comedy, call'd *Love for Love*.[8] Those Excellent Players,

---

[6] *Pall-Mall:* A fashionable street in London near St. James's Park famous for its expensive shops, elegant residences, coffeehouses, and clubs.

[7] *Mr. Betterton:* Thomas Betterton (1635–1710) was the greatest actor of the Restoration period. He acted in 180 roles; at the time of this paper he was over seventy years old and died the following April. Steele publishes a eulogy for him in *Tatler* No. 167.

[8] *Love for Love:* A play by William Congreve (1670–1729), an English neoclassical dramatist best known for his comedies of manners.

Mrs. *Barry*, Mrs. *Bracegirdle*, and Mr. *Dogget*,[9] tho' not at present concern'd in the House, acted on that Occasion. There has not been known so great a Concourse of Persons of Distinction as at that Time; the Stage it self was cover'd with Gentlemen and Ladies, and when the Curtain was drawn, it discovered even there a very splendid Audience. This unusual Encouragement which was given to a Play for the Advantage of so Great an Actor, gives an undeniable Instance, That the True Relish for Manly Entertainment and Rational Pleasures is not wholly lost. All the Parts were acted to Perfection; the Actors were careful of their Carriage, and no one was guilty of the Affection to insert Witticisms of his own, but a due Respect was had to the Audience, for encouraging this accomplish'd Player. It is not now doubted but Plays will revive, and take their usual Place in the Opinion of Persons of Wit and Merit, notwithstanding their late Apostacy in Favour of Dress and Sound. This Place[10] is very much alter'd since Mr. *Dryden*[11] frequented it; where you us'd to see *Songs, Epigrams,* and *Satyrs,* in the Hands of every Man you met, you have now only a Pack of Cards; and instead of the Cavils about the Turn of the Expression, the Elegance of the Style, and the like, the Learned now dispute only about the Truth of the Game. But, however the Company is alter'd, all have shewn a great Respect for Mr. *Betterton*; and the very Gaming Part of this House have been so much touch'd with a Sence of the Uncertainty of Humane Affairs, (which alter with themselves every Moment) that in this Gentleman, they pitied *Mark Anthony* of *Rome, Hamlett* of *Denmark, Mithridates* of *Pontus, Theodosius* of *Greece,* and *Henry* the Eighth of *England*. It is well known, he has been in the Condition of each of those illustrious Personages for several Hours together, and behav'd himself in those high Stations, in all the Changes of the Scene, with suitable Dignity. For these Reasons, we intend to repeat this Favour to him on a proper Occasion, lest he who can instruct us so well in personating Feigned Sor-

---

[9] *Mrs. Barry, Mrs. Bracegirdle, and Mr. Dogget:* One of the chief actresses in both comic and tragic roles, Elizabeth Barry (1658–1713) was at this time nearing the end of her acting career. Anne Bracegirdle (1663–1748) was a celebrated actress and singer who starred in many of Congreve's productions. Thomas Doggett (1670–1721) was a Dublin-born comic actor and joint manager with Colley Cibber of the Haymarket Theatre and later of the Drury Lane Theatre.

[10] *This Place:* Will's Coffee-house.

[11] *Mr. Dryden:* John Dryden (1631–1700) was a poet, playwright, essayist, and translator. He wrote both comedies, such as *Marriage à la Mode,* and heroic tragedies, like *Don Sebastian*. A famous Tory satirist, Dryden's most important work in this mode appeared in the 1680s and includes *MacFlecknoe* and *Absalom and Achitophel*.

rows, should be lost to us by suffering under Real Ones. The Town is at present in very great Expectation of seeing a Comedy now in Rehearsal, which is the 25th Production of my Honour'd Friend Mr. *Thomas D'Urfey*;[12] who, besides his great Abilities in the Dramatick, has a peculiar Talent in the Lyrick Way of Writing, and that with a Manner wholly new and unknown to the Antient *Greeks* and *Romans*, wherein he is but faintly imitated in the Translations of the Modern *Italian* Opera's.

St. James's Coffee-house, April 11.

Letters from the *Hague*[13] of the 16th, say, That Major General *Cadogan* was gone to *Brussels*, with Orders to disperse proper Instructions for assembling the whole Force of the Allies in *Flanders* in the Beginning of the next Month. The late Offers concerning Peace, were made in the Style of Persons who think themselves upon equal Terms: But the Allies have so just a Sense of their present Advantages, that they will not admit of a Treaty, except *France* offers what is more suitable to her present Condition. At the same Time we make Preparations, as if we were alarm'd by a greater Force than that which we are carrying into the Field. Thus this Point seems now to be argued Sword in Hand. This was what a Great General alluded to, when being ask'd the Names of those who were to be Plenipotentiaries for the ensuing Peace; answer'd, with a serious Air, *There are about an Hundred thousand of us.* Mr. *Kidney*, who has the Ear of the Greatest Politicians that come hither, tells me, There is a Mail come in to Day with Letters, dated *Hague, April* 19, N.S. which say, a Design of bringing Part of our Troops into the Field at the latter End of this Month, is now alter'd to a Resolution of marching towards the Camp about the 20th of the next. There happen'd t'other Day, in the Road of *Scheveling*, an Engagement between a Privateer of *Zealand* and one of *Dunkirk*. The *Dunkirker*, carrying 33 Pieces of Cannon, was taken and brought into the *Texel*. It is said, the

---

[12] *Mr. Thomas D'Urfey:* Thomas D'Urfey (1653–1723) was a dramatist and satirist of French Huguenot descent. The production referred to here is a new comedy, *The Modern Prophets, or, New Wit for a Husband,* which was produced at Drury Lane the following month.

[13] *the Hague:* The capital of the Netherlands, which by the seventeenth century was Europe's principal diplomatic center. In the early eighteenth century the Netherlands was a major arena in England's war with France, the War of the Spanish Succession. During the course of the war, John Churchill, Duke of Marlborough (1650–1722), led English and Dutch armies against French forces in ten campaigns there.

Courier of Monsieur *Rouillé* is return'd to him from the Court of *France*. Monsieur *Vendosme* being reinstated in the Favour of the Dutchess of *Burgundy*, is to command in *Flanders*.

Mr. *Kidney* added, that there were Letters of the 17th from *Ghent*, which give an Account, that the Enemy had form'd a Design to surprise two Battalions of the Allies which lay at *Alost*; but those Battalions receiv'd Advice of their March, and retir'd to *Dendermond*. Lieutenant General *Wood* appear'd on this Occasion at the Head of 5000 Foot and 1000 Horse, upon which the Enemy withdrew without making any further Attempt.

From my own Apartment.

I am sorry I am obliged to trouble the Publick with so much Discourse, upon a Matter which I at the very first mentioned as a Trifle, *viz.* the Death of Mr. *Partridge*, under whose Name there is an *Almanack*[14] come out for the Year 1709. In one Page of which, it is asserted by the said *John Partridge*, That he is still living, and not only so, but that he was also living some Time before, and even at the Instant when I writ of his Death. I have in another Place, and in a Paper by it self, sufficiently convinc'd this Man that he is dead, and if he has any Shame, I don't doubt but that by this Time he owns it to all his Acquaintance: For tho' the Legs and Arms, and whole Body, of that Man may still appear and perform their animal Functions; yet since, as I have elsewhere observ'd, his Art is gone, the Man is gone. I am, as I said, concern'd, that this little Matter should make so much Noise; but since I am engag'd, I take my self oblig'd in Honour to go on in my Lucubrations, and by the Help of these Arts of which I am Master, as well as my Skill in Astrological Speculations, I shall, as I see Occasion, proceed to confute other dead Men, who pretend to be in Being, that they are actually deceased. I therefore give all Men fair Warning to mend their Manners, for I shall from Time to Time print Bills of Mortality; and I beg the Pardon of all such who shall be nam'd therein, if they who are good for Nothing shall find themselves in the Number of the Deceased.

---

[14] *Mr. Partridge . . . an Almanack:* For the satiric contest between Isaac Bickerstaff and John Partridge see the Introduction to this volume. The almanac here referred to is *Merlinus Liberatus*, Partridge's almanac for 1709 in which he protests that he is "still alive."

No. 144
Saturday, March 11, 1710
[Steele as Isaac Bickerstaff, "Censor of Great Britain"]

Sheer-Lane, March 10.

In a Nation of Liberty, there is hardly a Person in the whole Mass of the People more absolutely necessary than a Censor.[1] It is allowed, that I have no Authority for assuming this important Appellation; and that I am Censor of these Nations, just as one is chosen King at the Game of Questions and Commands.[2] But if in the Execution of this fantastical Dignity, I observe upon Things which do not fall within the Cognizance of real Authority, I hope it will be granted, that an idle Man could not be more usefully employed. Among all the Irregularities of which I have taken Notice, I know none so proper to be presented to the World by a Censor, as that of the general Expence and Affectation in Equipage. I have lately hinted, that this Extravagance must necessarily get Footing where we have no Sumptuary Laws, and where every Man may be dressed, attended, and carried in what Manner he pleases: But my Tenderness to my Fellow Subjects will not permit me to let this Enormity go unobserved.

As the Matter now stands, every Man takes it in his Head, That he has a Liberty to spend his Money as he pleases. Thus, in Spight of all Order, Justice and Decorum, we the greater Number of the Queen's loyal Subjects, for no Reason in the World but because we want Money, do not share alike in the Division of Her Majesty's High Road. The Horses and Slaves of the Rich take up the whole Street, while we Peripateticks[3] are very glad to watch Opportunity to whisk cross a Passage, very thankful that we are not run over for interrupting the Machine, that carries in it a Person neither more handsome, wise, or valiant, than the meanest of us. For this Reason, were I to propose a Tax, it should certainly be upon Coaches and Chairs;[4] for no Man living can assign a Reason why one Man should have half a

---

[1] *Censor:* In ancient Rome the censor was an official in charge of taking population counts and correcting morals.

[2] *Game of Questions and Commands:* A popular parlor game (like today's Truth or Dare).

[3] *Peripateticks:* The Peripatetics were a group of Aristotelian philosophers in ancient Greece. They were so called because they followed the teaching style of Greek philosopher Aristotle (384–322 B.C.), who walked around (in Greek, *peripatein*) while lecturing at the Lyceum.

[4] *Chairs:* Sedan chairs, in which people were carried through the streets.

Street to carry him at his Ease, and perhaps only in Pursuit of Pleasures, when as good a Man as himself wants Room for his own Person to pass upon the most necessary and urgent Occasion. Till such
an Acknowledgment is made to the Publick, I shall take upon me to
vest certain Rights in the Scavengers of the Cities of *London* and
Westminister, to take the Horses and Servants of all such as do not
become or deserve such Distinctions into their peculiar Custody. The
Offenders themselves I shall allow safe Conduct to their Places of
Abode in the Carts of the said Scavengers, but their Horses shall be
mounted by their Footmen, and sent into the Service Abroad. And I
take this Opportunity in the first Place to recruit the Regiment of
my good old Friend the brave and honest *Sylvius*, that they be as
well taught as they are fed. It is to me most miraculous, so unreason-
able an Usurpation as this I am speaking of should so long have
been tolerated. We hang a poor Fellow for taking any Trifle from
us on the Road, and bear with the Rich for robbing us of the Road
it self. Such a Tax as this would be of great Satisfaction to us who
walk on Foot; and since the Distinction of riding in a Coach is not
to be appointed according to a Man's Merit, or Service to their
Country, nor that Liberty given as a Reward for some eminent
Virtue, we should be highly contented to see them pay something for
the Insult they do us in the State they take upon them while they are
drawn by us.

Till they have made us some Reparation of this kind, we the Peripateticks of *Great Britain* cannot think our selves well treated, while
every one that is able is allowed to set up an Equipage.

As for my Part, I cannot but admire how Persons, conscious to
themselves of no manner of Superiority above others, can out of meer
Pride or Laziness expose themselves at this Rate to publick View, and
put us all upon pronouncing those Three terrible Syllables, Who is
that? When it comes to that Question, our Method is to consider the
Mien and Air of the Passenger, and comfort our selves for being dirty
to the Ankles by laughing at his Figure and Appearance who over-
looks us. I must confess, were it not for the solid Injustice of the
Thing, there is nothing could afford a discerning Eye greater Occasion for Mirth than this licentious Huddle of Qualities and Characters in the Equipages about this Town. The Overseers of the Highway
and Constables have so little Skill or Power to rectify this Matter,
that you may often see the Equipage of a Fellow whom all the Town
knows to deserve hanging, make a Stop that shall interrupt the Lord
High Chancellor and all the Judges in their Way to *Westminister*.

rince, which Time will bring to Light. Now the *Post-Man*, says he, who uses to be very clear, refers to the same News in these Words; *The late Conduct of a certain Prince affords great Matter of Specula-tion.* This certain Prince, says the Upholsterer, whom they are all so cautious of naming, I take to be — Upon which, tho' there was no boy near us, he whispered something in my Ear, which I did not he, or think worth my while to make him repeat.

e were now got to the upper End of the *Mall*,[8] where were Three our very odd Fellows sitting together upon the Bench. These I f were all of them Politicians, who used to Sun themselves in ace every Day about Dinner-Time. Observing them to be Cu- in their Kind, and my Friend's Acquaintance, I sat down hem.

hief Politician of the Bench was a great Asserter of Para- e told us, with a seeming Concern, That by some News he read from *Muscovy*, it appeared to him that there was a ering in the Black Sea, which might in Time do Hurt to the es of this Nation. To this he added, That for his Part, he ish to see the Turk driven out of *Europe*, which he be- not but be prejudicial to our Woollen Manufacture. He That he looked upon these extraordinary Revolutions ly happened in these Parts of the World, to have risen wo Persons who were not much talked of; and those, ince *Menzikoff*, and the Dutchess of *Mirandola*. He tions with so many broken Hints, and such a Show sdom, that we gave our selves up to his Opinions. at length fell upon a Point which seldom escapes a *Englishmen*, Whether in Case of a Religious War, uld not be too strong for the Papists? This we mined on the Protestant Side. One who sat on my I found by his Discourse, had been in the *West-* That it would be a very easie Matter for the e Pope at Sea; and added, That whenever such a must turn to the Good of the *Leeward* Islands. t at the End of the Bench, and, as I afterwards pher of the Company, said, That in case the Protestants from these Parts of *Europe*, when

for a half-mile along the north border of St. James's

For the better understanding of Things and Persons in this general Confusion, I have given Directions to all the Coach-Makers and Coach-Painters in Town to bring me in Lists of their several Customers; and doubt not, but with comparing the Orders of each Man in the placing his Arms on the Doors of his Chariot, as well as the Words, Devices, and Cyphers, to be fixed upon them, to make a Collection, which shall let us into the Nature, if not the History, of Mankind, more usefully than the Curiosities of any Medallist in *Europe*.

But this Evil of Vanity in our Figure, with many many others, proceeds from a certain Gaiety of Heart which has crept into Men's very Thoughts and Complexions. The Passions and Adventures of Heroes, when they enter the Lists for the Tournament in Romances, are not more easily distinguishable by their Palfries and their Armour, than the secret Springs and Affections of the several Pretenders to Show amongst us are known by their Equipages in ordinary Life. The young Bridegroom with his gilded Cupids and winged Angels, has some Excuse in the Joy of his Heart to launch out into something that may be significant of his present Happiness; but to see Men for no Reason upon Earth but that they are rich, ascend to triumphant Chariots, and ride through the People, has at the Bottom nothing else in it but an insolent Transport, arising only from the Distinction of Fortune.

It is therefore high Time that I call in such Coaches as are in their Embellishments improper for the Character of their Owners: But if I find I am not obeyed herein, and that I cannot pull down these Equipages already erected, I shall take upon me to prevent the Growth of this Evil for the future, by enquiring into the Pretensions of the Persons who shall hereafter attempt to make publick Entries, with Ornaments and Decorations of their own Appointment. If a Man who believed he had the handsomest Leg in this Kingdom, should take a Fancy to adorn so deserving a Limb with a blue Garter, he would justly be punished for offending against the most noble Order; and, I think, the general Prostitution of Equipage and Retinue is as destructive to all Distinction, as the Impertinence of one Man, if permitted, would certainly be to that illustrious Fraternity.

ADVERTISEMENT.

The Censor having lately received Intelligence, that the ancient Simplicity in the Dress and Manners of that Part of this Island, called Scotland, *begins to decay; and that there are at this Time, in the good*

Town of Edinburgh, *Beaus, Fops and Coxcombs: His late Correspondent from that Place is desired to send up their Names and Characingly, and proper Officers named to take in their Canes, Snuff-Boxes, and all other useless Necessaries commonly worn by such Offenders.*

No. 155
Thursday, April 6, 1710
[Addison on the Political Upholsterer Addicted to News]

—— *Aliena Negotia curat*
Excussus propriis.[1]

— Hor.

From my own Apartment, April 5.

There lived some Years since within my Neighbourhood a very grave Person, an Upholsterer, who seemed a Man of more than ordinary Application to Business. He was a very early Riser, and was often abroad Two or Three Hours before any of his Neighbours. He had a particular Carefulness in the knitting of his Brows, and a kind of Impatience in all his Motions, that plainly discovered he was always intent on Matters of Importance. Upon my Enquiry into his Life and Conversation, I found him to be the greatest Newsmonger in our Quarter; that he rose before Day to read the *Post-Man*[2] and that he would take Two or Three Turns to the other End of the Town before his Neighbours were up, to see if there were any *Dutch* Mails come in. He had a Wife and several Children; but was much more inquisitive to know what passes in *Poland* than in his own Family, and was in greater Pain and Anxiety of Mind for King *Augustus*'s Welfare[3] than that of his nearest Relations. He looked extremely thin in a Dearth of News, and never enjoyed himself in a Westerly Wind. This indefatigable kind of Life was the Ruin of his Shop; for about the

[1] *Aliena . . . propriis:* From Horace, *Satires* 2.3.19–20 (altered): "He minds others' concerns, since he has lost his own" [Bond].
[2] *Post-Man:* The leading Whig newspaper.
[3] *King Augustus's Welfare:* Frederick Augustus I, Elector of Saxony (1670–1733), was elected King August II of Poland in 1696. With Peter I of Russia and Christian V of Denmark, he formed a coalition against King Charles XII of Sweden in the Great Northern War (1700–21).

Time that his favourite Prince left the Crown of *Poland*, he disappeared.

This Man and his Affairs had been long out of my Mind, Three Days ago, as I was walking in St. *James*'s Park, I he body at a Distance hemming after me: And who should it old Neighbour the Upholsterer? I saw he was reduced to Poverty, by certain shabby Superfluities in his Dress: For standing that it was a very sultry Day for the Time of the wore a loose great Coat and a Muff, with a long Campagne of Curl; to which he had added the Ornament of a Pair Garters buckled under the Knee. Upon his coming up to going to enquire into his present Circumstances; but wa by his asking me, with a Whisper, Whether the last Le any Accounts that one might rely upon from *Bende* None that I heard of; and asked him, Whether he had eldest Daughter? He told me, No. But pray, says he, What are your Thoughts of the King of *Sweden*?[4] and Children were starving, I found his chief Conce for this great Monarch. I told him, That I looked the first Heroes of the Age. But pray, says he, any thing in the Story of his Wound? And findi Question, Nay, says he, I only propose it to thought there was no Reason to doubt of it. he, more than in any other Part of the Body let chanced to light there.

This extraordinary Dialogue was no s launch out into a long Dissertation up and after having spent some Time on great Perplexity how to reconcile the *Post*,[5] and had been just now exam upon the same Subject. The *Daily-* *We have Advices from very goo* *some Matters of great Importa* mysterious; but the *Post-Boy* us, *That there are private I*

[4] *King of Sweden:* Charles
his country in the Great Nort
[5] *the Supplement with*
leading Tory newspaper)
probably the *Evening Po*
[6] *a certain Prince:*
[7] *the Post-Boy:* T'

For the better understanding of Things and Persons in this general Confusion, I have given Directions to all the Coach-Makers and Coach-Painters in Town to bring me in Lists of their several Customers; and doubt not, but with comparing the Orders of each Man in the placing his Arms on the Doors of his Chariot, as well as the Words, Devices, and Cyphers, to be fixed upon them, to make a Collection, which shall let us into the Nature, if not the History, of Mankind, more usefully than the Curiosities of any Medallist in *Europe*.

But this Evil of Vanity in our Figure, with many many others, proceeds from a certain Gaiety of Heart which has crept into Men's very Thoughts and Complexions. The Passions and Adventures of Heroes, when they enter the Lists for the Tournament in Romances, are not more easily distinguishable by their Palfries and their Armour, than the secret Springs and Affections of the several Pretenders to Show amongst us are known by their Equipages in ordinary Life. The young Bridegroom with his gilded Cupids and winged Angels, has some Excuse in the Joy of his Heart to launch out into something that may be significant of his present Happiness; but to see Men for no Reason upon Earth but that they are rich, ascend to triumphant Chariots, and ride through the People, has at the Bottom nothing else in it but an insolent Transport, arising only from the Distinction of Fortune.

It is therefore high Time that I call in such Coaches as are in their Embellishments improper for the Character of their Owners: But if I find I am not obeyed herein, and that I cannot pull down these Equipages already erected, I shall take upon me to prevent the Growth of this Evil for the future, by enquiring into the Pretensions of the Persons who shall hereafter attempt to make publick Entries, with Ornaments and Decorations of their own Appointment. If a Man who believed he had the handsomest Leg in this Kingdom, should take a Fancy to adorn so deserving a Limb with a blue Garter, he would justly be punished for offending against the most noble Order; and, I think, the general Prostitution of Equipage and Retinue is as destructive to all Distinction, as the Impertinence of one Man, if permitted, would certainly be to that illustrious Fraternity.

ADVERTISEMENT.

The Censor having lately received Intelligence, that the ancient Simplicity in the Dress and Manners of that Part of this Island, called Scotland, *begins to decay; and that there are at this Time, in the good*

Town of Edinburgh, Beaus, Fops and Coxcombs: His late Correspondent from that Place is desired to send up their Names and Characters with all Expedition, that they may be proceeded against accordingly, and proper Officers named to take in their Canes, Snuff-Boxes, and all other useless Necessaries commonly worn by such Offenders.

No. 155
Thursday, April 6, 1710
[Addison on the Political Upholsterer Addicted to News]

—— *Aliena Negotia curat*
Excussus propriis.[1]
— Hor.

From my own Apartment, April 5.

There lived some Years since within my Neighbourhood a very grave Person, an Upholsterer, who seemed a Man of more than ordinary Application to Business. He was a very early Riser, and was often abroad Two or Three Hours before any of his Neighbours. He had a particular Carefulness in the knitting of his Brows, and a kind of Impatience in all his Motions, that plainly discovered he was always intent on Matters of Importance. Upon my Enquiry into his Life and Conversation, I found him to be the greatest Newsmonger in our Quarter; that he rose before Day to read the *Post-Man*[2] and that he would take Two or Three Turns to the other End of the Town before his Neighbours were up, to see if there were any *Dutch* Mails come in. He had a Wife and several Children; but was much more inquisitive to know what passes in *Poland* than in his own Family, and was in greater Pain and Anxiety of Mind for King *Augustus*'s Welfare[3] than that of his nearest Relations. He looked extremely thin in a Dearth of News, and never enjoyed himself in a Westerly Wind. This indefatigable kind of Life was the Ruin of his Shop; for about the

[1] *Aliena . . . propriis:* From Horace, *Satires* 2.3.19–20 (altered): "He minds others' concerns, since he has lost his own" [Bond].

[2] *Post-Man:* The leading Whig newspaper.

[3] *King Augustus's Welfare:* Frederick Augustus I, Elector of Saxony (1670–1733), was elected King August II of Poland in 1696. With Peter I of Russia and Christian V of Denmark, he formed a coalition against King Charles XII of Sweden in the Great Northern War (1700–21).

Time that his favourite Prince left the Crown of *Poland*, he broke and disappeared.

This Man and his Affairs had been long out of my Mind, till about Three Days ago, as I was walking in St. *James*'s Park, I heard some body at a Distance hemming after me: And who should it be but my old Neighbour the Upholsterer? I saw he was reduced to extreme Poverty, by certain shabby Superfluities in his Dress: For notwithstanding that it was a very sultry Day for the Time of the Year, he wore a loose great Coat and a Muff, with a long Campagne-Wig out of Curl; to which he had added the Ornament of a Pair of black Garters buckled under the Knee. Upon his coming up to me, I was going to enquire into his present Circumstances; but was prevented by his asking me, with a Whisper, Whether the last Letters brought any Accounts that one might rely upon from *Bender*? I told him, None that I heard of; and asked him, Whether he had yet married his eldest Daughter? He told me, No. But pray, says he, tell me sincerely, What are your Thoughts of the King of *Sweden*?[4] For tho' his Wife and Children were starving, I found his chief Concern at present was for this great Monarch. I told him, That I looked upon him as one of the first Heroes of the Age. But pray, says he, do you think there is any thing in the Story of his Wound? And finding me surprised at the Question, Nay, says he, I only propose it to you. I answered, That I thought there was no Reason to doubt of it. But why in the Heel, says he, more than in any other Part of the Body? Because, says I, the Bullet chanced to light there.

This extraordinary Dialogue was no sooner ended, but he began to launch out into a long Dissertation upon the Affairs of the *North*; and after having spent some Time on them, he told me, He was in a great Perplexity how to reconcile the *Supplement* with the *English-Post*,[5] and had been just now examining what the other Papers say upon the same Subject. The *Daily-Courant*, says he, has these Words, *We have Advices from very good Hands, That a certain Prince*[6] *has some Matters of great Importance under Consideration.* This is very mysterious; but the *Post-Boy*[7] leaves us more in the Dark, for he tells us, *That there are private Intimations of Measures taken by a certain*

---

[4] *King of Sweden:* Charles XII of Sweden (1682–1718) was a military hero who led his country in the Great Northern War.

[5] *the Supplement with the English-Post:* The *Supplement* (to the *Post-Boy*, the leading Tory newspaper) had begun publication in January 1708; the *English-Post* was probably the *Evening Post*, begun in September 1709 [Bond].

[6] *a certain Prince:* Charles XII of Sweden.

[7] *the Post-Boy:* The leading Tory newspaper, not to be confused with the *Post-Man*.

Prince, which Time will bring to Light. Now the *Post-Man*, says he, who uses to be very clear, refers to the same News in these Words; *The late Conduct of a certain Prince affords great Matter of Speculation.* This certain Prince, says the Upholsterer, whom they are all so cautious of naming, I take to be — Upon which, tho' there was no body near us, he whispered something in my Ear, which I did not hear, or think worth my while to make him repeat.

We were now got to the upper End of the *Mall*,[8] where were Three or Four very odd Fellows sitting together upon the Bench. These I found were all of them Politicians, who used to Sun themselves in that Place every Day about Dinner-Time. Observing them to be Curiosities in their Kind, and my Friend's Acquaintance, I sat down among them.

The chief Politician of the Bench was a great Asserter of Paradoxes. He told us, with a seeming Concern, That by some News he had lately read from *Muscovy*, it appeared to him that there was a Storm gathering in the Black Sea, which might in Time do Hurt to the Naval Forces of this Nation. To this he added, That for his Part, he could not wish to see the Turk driven out of *Europe*, which he believed could not but be prejudicial to our Woollen Manufacture. He then told us, That he looked upon these extraordinary Revolutions which had lately happened in these Parts of the World, to have risen chiefly from Two Persons who were not much talked of; and those, says he, are Prince *Menzikoff*, and the Dutchess of *Mirandola*. He back'd his Assertions with so many broken Hints, and such a Show of Depth and Wisdom, that we gave our selves up to his Opinions.

The Discourse at length fell upon a Point which seldom escapes a Knot of true-born *Englishmen*, Whether in Case of a Religious War, the Protestants would not be too strong for the Papists? This we unanimously determined on the Protestant Side. One who sat on my Right Hand, and, as I found by his Discourse, had been in the *West-Indies*, assured us, That it would be a very easie Matter for the Protestants to beat the Pope at Sea; and added, That whenever such a War does break out, it must turn to the Good of the *Leeward* Islands. Upon this, one who sat at the End of the Bench, and, as I afterwards found, was the Geographer of the Company, said, That in case the Papists should drive the Protestants from these Parts of *Europe*, when

---

[8] *the Mall*: A walk that ran for a half-mile along the north border of St. James's Park.